Year-Round Grilling

Jean Paré

companyscoming.com
visit our ↖website

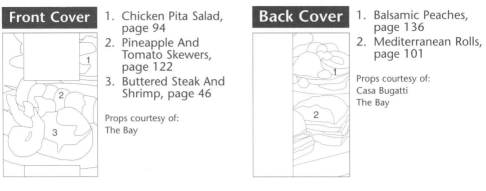

Front Cover
1. Chicken Pita Salad, page 94
2. Pineapple And Tomato Skewers, page 122
3. Buttered Steak And Shrimp, page 46

Props courtesy of:
The Bay

Back Cover
1. Balsamic Peaches, page 136
2. Mediterranean Rolls, page 101

Props courtesy of:
Casa Bugatti
The Bay

We gratefully acknowledge the following suppliers for their generous support of our Test Kitchen and Photo Studio:

Broil King Barbecues®   *Lagostina®*
Corelle®   *Proctor Silex® Canada*
Hamilton Beach® Canada   *Tupperware®*

Year-Round Grilling

Fourth Printing November 2005

Library and Archives Canada Cataloguing in Publication
Paré, Jean, date
Company's coming, year-round grilling / Jean Paré.
(Original series)
ISBN 1-896891-52-7
1. Barbecue cookery. I. Title. II. Series: Paré, Jean. Original series.
TX840.B3P374 2003   641.7'6   C2002-904924-5

Published by
Company's Coming Publishing Limited
2311 – 96 Street
Edmonton, Alberta, Canada T6N 1G3
Tel: 780-450-6223   Fax: 780-450-1857
www.companyscoming.com

Printed in Canada

Need more recipes?

Six "**sneak preview**" recipes are featured online with every new book released.

Visit us at

www.companyscoming.com

Company's Coming Cookbooks

Original Series

- Softcover, 160 pages
- 6" x 9" (15 cm x 23 cm) format
- Lay-flat plastic comb binding
- Full-colour photos
- Nutrition information

Quick & easy recipes! Everyday ingredients!

Lifestyle Series

- Softcover, 160 pages
- 8" x 10" (20 cm x 25 cm) format
- Paperback
- Full-colour photos
- Nutrition information

Most Loved Recipe Collection

- Hardcover, 128 pages
- 8 3/4" x 8 3/4" (22 cm x 22 cm) format
- Durable sewn binding
- Full colour throughout
- Nutrition information

Special Occasion Series

- Hardcover & softcover, 192 pages
- 8 1/2" x 11" (22 cm x 28 cm) format
- Durable sewn binding
- Full colour throughout
- Nutrition information

See page 157 for more cookbooks.
For a complete listing, visit
www.companyscoming.com

Table of Contents

Basics of Grilling

Marinating Magic

Appetizers

Breads

Smoked Dishes

Desserts

Recipe Index

The Company's Coming Story

Jean Paré (pronounced "jeen PAIR-ee") grew up understanding that the combination of family, friends and home cooking is the best recipe for a good life. From her mother, she learned to appreciate good cooking, while her father praised even her earliest attempts in the kitchen. When Jean left home, she took with her a love of cooking, many family recipes and an intriguing desire to read cookbooks as if they were novels!

"never share a recipe you wouldn't use yourself"

In 1963, when her four children had all reached school age, Jean volunteered to cater the 50th Anniversary of the Vermilion School of Agriculture, now Lakeland College, in Alberta, Canada. Working out of her home, Jean prepared a dinner for more than 1,000 people, which launched a flourishing catering operation that continued for over 18 years. During that time, she had countless opportunities to test new ideas with immediate feedback—resulting in empty plates and contented customers! Whether preparing cocktail sandwiches for a house party or serving a hot meal for 1,500 people, Jean Paré earned a reputation for good food, courteous service and reasonable prices.

As requests for her recipes mounted, Jean was often asked the question, "Why don't you write a cookbook?" Jean responded by teaming up with her son, Grant Lovig, in the fall of 1980 to form Company's Coming Publishing Limited. The publication of *150 Delicious Squares* on April 14, 1981 marked the debut of what would soon become one of the world's most popular cookbook series.

The company has grown since those early days when Jean worked from a spare bedroom in her home. Today, she continues to write recipes while working closely with the staff of the Recipe Factory, as the Company's Coming test kitchen is affectionately known. There she fills the role of mentor, assisting with the development of recipes people most want to use for everyday cooking and easy entertaining. Every Company's Coming recipe is *kitchen-tested* before it's approved for publication.

Jean's daughter, Gail Lovig, is responsible for marketing and distribution, leading a team that includes sales personnel located in major cities across Canada. In addition, Company's Coming cookbooks are published and

distributed under licence in the United States, Australia and other world markets. Bestsellers many times over in English, Company's Coming cookbooks have also been published in French and Spanish.

Familiar and trusted in home kitchens around the world, Company's Coming cookbooks are offered in a variety of formats. Highly regarded as kitchen workbooks, the softcover Original Series, with its lay-flat plastic comb binding, is still a favourite among readers.

Jean Paré's approach to cooking has always called for *quick and easy recipes* using *everyday ingredients*. That view has served her well. The recipient of many awards, including the Queen Elizabeth Golden Jubilee medal, Jean was appointed a Member of the Order of Canada, her country's highest lifetime achievement honour.

Jean continues to gain new supporters by adhering to what she calls The Golden Rule of Cooking: *"Never share a recipe you wouldn't use yourself."* It's an approach that works—*millions of times over!*

Foreword

There is something tantalizing about the taste of food cooked on the grill. Perhaps it's the delicious smoky flavour combined with the enticing sizzle of juices. Or maybe it's the fact that grilling allows us to capture that carefree summertime feeling of enjoying great food with friends and family.

It used to be that we only made use of our charcoal barbecues during the short summer season. Then they would be covered up—a sure sign that winter was coming. Today, we enjoy grilling all year round!

Indoor electric grills and outdoor gas barbecues are becoming more and more popular—and for good reason. Grilling not only makes food taste great, it's also a healthy, low-fat way to prepare our favourite meals. In recent years, grilling has become easier and a great deal safer than it used to be. Unless we choose to, we no longer have to fuss with charcoal bricks, lighter fluid or matches. With the convenience of new designs and technology, grilling is now as easy as flicking a switch!

The growing popularity of grilling encouraged us to create this cookbook filled with indoor grill and barbecue recipes that can be enjoyed any time of year. In *Year-Round Grilling*, you will find a collection of fabulous recipes for the barbecue as well as for the single and two-sided electric grills. We've included recipes for easy-to-prepare appetizers, entrees, vegetable dishes and even desserts. You'll be surprised and delighted by the versatility of your grill. Soon you'll be using it for a lot more than hamburgers and steaks! Who would have imagined how delicious grilled fruit kabobs

could be? And grilled vegetables offer a tasty change from traditional steamed vegetables.

We have also included some useful information about grilling. You will find some great tips for marinating and some fabulous marinade recipes that will really bring out the flavour of your grilled dishes.

With *Year-Round Grilling*, you can enjoy great food and that carefree feeling of summer all year long!

Jean Paré

Each recipe has been analyzed using the most up-to-date version of the Canadian Nutrient File from Health Canada, which is based on the United States Department of Agriculture (USDA) Nutrient Data Base. If more than one ingredient is listed (such as "hard margarine or butter"), or a range is given (1 – 2 tsp., 5 – 10 mL) then the first ingredient or amount is used in the analysis. Where an ingredient reads "sprinkle," "optional," or "for garnish," it is not included as part of the nutrition information. Milk, unless stated otherwise, is 1% and cooking oil, unless stated otherwise, is canola.

Margaret Ng, B.Sc. (Hon), M.A.
Registered Dietitian

Basics of Grilling

Grilling is a year-round activity that can be done indoors or outdoors. While the art of grilling goes back thousands of years, the tools we use to grill food are constantly evolving to suit the needs of each new generation. Today, there is a mixture of traditional and modern grills on the market. *Year-Round Grilling* focuses on the indoor electric grill and the outdoor gas barbecue. As the popularity of indoor grilling grows, many households will have the advantage of being able to use both methods.

Should we "grill" or "barbecue?"....

Is it "grill and grilling" or "barbecue and barbecuing?" Are they nouns? Verbs? The same? Different? These terms are pretty much synonymous and interchangeable with one another. Even reading the definitions in the dictionary doesn't make the distinction much clearer. Basically, barbecuing, or food done in a barbecue, is usually assumed to be over a charcoal or gas heat source; grilling is over any heat source. In both cases, the food is placed on a series of metal bars. In *Year-Round Grilling*, we have chosen to use "grilling" as our preferred verb. We have only used the term "barbecue" as a noun in reference to the outdoor gas appliance that the majority of us now use.

Electric Indoor Grills

Electric grills are gaining in popularity each year and have greatly added to the enjoyment of apartment and condo dwellers. Being able to duplicate the speed, flavour and look of outdoor barbecuing, without having to risk poor weather conditions and an empty propane tank, is appealing to more and more cooks.

There are a number of different models available, each with varying features. These are some of the most common:

1. One side only with no variable temperature (just on and off) and no optional flat griddle surface.

2. One side only with variable temperature and a flat griddle surface at the side for frying.

3. Two sides, hinged (food is grilled on both sides at the same time), with no variable temperature (just on and off) and no optional flat griddle surface.

Indoor grills are best suited for cooking smaller quantities of food as their surface area is about one-third of an outdoor barbecue. As well, foods with sugar-based marinades are not advised on the indoor grill because of the potential for smoke.

Outdoor Gas Barbecues

Adventurous outdoor chefs have a variety of cooking options available to them. From potatoes nestled in the smouldering wood fire to steaks sizzling under the lid of the gas barbecue, they can choose their preferred cooking method. However, a gas barbecue offers the convenience of quick and even heat, and can be adjusted to cook at any temperature. Propane or natural gas heats up lava rocks, ceramic briquettes or flavour bars, which in turn do a quick and efficient job of radiating heat.

Cooking Methods

Direct Heat Cooking: Food is cooked directly over the heat source. This method cooks the food quickly and is best suited to smaller or individual items such as steaks, chicken breasts, kabobs, burgers and vegetables.

Indirect Heat Cooking: The heat source is around the food rather than directly under it. This cooking method is only possible with the outdoor barbecue. Turn off either the left or centre burner after preheating. Place the food over the burner that has been turned off. Place a drip pan (see Tip, page 76) under the food and close the lid. This process works for roasts, ribs and other larger, less tender cuts of meat.

Common Grilling Terms

Baste: To brush or dab food with a liquid, such as a marinade, sauce or butter, during cooking either to help keep food moist, add flavour or make an attractive glaze on the surface of the food.

Blanch (parboil): To partially cook a vegetable by immersing in boiling water for a few seconds to several minutes then removing immediately and plunging into ice water to stop any further cooking. Blanching certain vegetables prior to placing on the grill will ensure that they will be thoroughly cooked without burning.

Butterfly: To slice a solid piece of meat, such as a boneless chicken breast, pork tenderloin and even large shrimp, horizontally down the centre almost all the way through. The two halves open out to resemble a butterfly. This provides a more even thickness for grilling.

Glaze: To coat food with a thin, glossy mixture by basting or brushing it on during the last few minutes of cooking. The coating usually contains some form of sugar (granulated, brown, corn syrup, etc.) so the food should be watched carefully on the grill to avoid burning.

Marinate: To immerse meat, fish, seafood, poultry, or even vegetables, in a liquid (generally acidic based) for an extended period of time (15 minutes to 1 day) to allow food to absorb the flavours and, in most cases, to tenderize.

Food Safety Tips

Warm summer months may be a great time to fire up the barbecue, but it's also a tricky time to make certain that food is prepared, cooked and served safely. Hot weather can turn perfectly good food into poison, even on the car ride home from the grocery store.

- Use only fresh meat, fish and poultry that have not been allowed to warm prior to cooking. At the grocery store, select these items last and check that packaging is not damaged.

- Transport food in a cool environment—an air-conditioned car, insulated cooler or ice-packed bags. Don't place groceries in the trunk of the car.

- Thaw frozen foods, particularly meat, fish and poultry, in the refrigerator, not on the counter.

- Wash hands thoroughly in hot, soapy water before handling any food.

- Keep raw meat and its juices away from other foods—use a separate cutting board and knife, cleaning the board with a small amount of chlorine bleach after each use.

- Precook chicken or ribs immediately before grilling. Do not allow the meat to cool down in between.

- Keep hot foods hot and cold foods cold. Never leave food out in the sun. Wait until you are ready to eat before serving then set food out in shady areas.

- Cook ground beef thoroughly until no pink shows through (see Tip, page 28).

- Marinate foods in the refrigerator, never on the counter, if they have a long marinating time. If you plan to use the marinade to baste your food, first bring it to a rolling boil for 5 minutes to kill any bacteria.

- Don't judge doneness of meat by its colour—it can be deceiving. Use an instant-read meat thermometer to ensure that the centre of larger pieces of meat, fish and poultry is cooked.

Basics of Grilling

Marinating Magic

To marinate means to create a savoury, acidic liquid that your meat, vegetables, poultry or seafood will stand or soak in for a period of time to tenderize and retain juiciness, as well as to enrich flavours. How much marinade you need depends on the amount of food to be marinated. A good guide is to plan on making about 1/2 cup (125 mL) marinade for every 1 lb. (454 g) of food.

Key Ingredients:

1. At least one acidic ingredient (such as vinegar, wine, lemon juice or other citrus fruit juice) partially helps to tenderize otherwise tough cuts of meat by breaking down the sinewy protein fibres. This process also encourages the absorption of marinade into the food.

2. Cooking oil may or may not be added. While it adds moisture and helps to keep food from sticking to the grill during the cooking process, oil also adds fat grams so use cautiously.

3. A mixture of herbs, spices and other seasonings that will enhance the flavour are essential.

To Marinate:

1. Mix marinade ingredients in a non-metallic pan—ceramic or glass works best. A plastic container also works fine but could possibly stain. A heavy-duty, disposable plastic freezer bag may also be used and makes cleanup quick and easy. Regardless, the container should be large enough to lay meat or vegetables in a single layer, or to allow food to be stirred or turned.

2. Add the food and stir, or turn over, to coat thoroughly. Cover or seal tightly and place in the refrigerator. Stir or turn food occasionally during the suggested standing time. Tender cuts of meat, as well as poultry, fish and seafood, might require as little as 15 minutes to marinate. Less tender steaks or roasts may need to marinate overnight.

3. Remove the food from the marinade, letting excess liquid drip back into the container. You may even want to blot the food with paper towel.

4. Place food on the preheated grill.

5. You have three choices with the remaining marinade: discard, boil and use for basting the food during grilling, or reheat to a rolling boil for 5 minutes after marinating or basting to kill any bacteria from the uncooked meat, then serve as a sauce with the grilled food.

Red Pepper Bruschetta

Small pieces of toasted bread rounds topped with
sweet roasted peppers and feta cheese.

Medium red pepper, quartered	1	1
Medium yellow pepper, quartered	1	1
Finely chopped fresh parsley (or 1 1/2 tsp., 7 mL, flakes)	2 tbsp.	30 mL
Finely chopped red onion	2 tbsp.	30 mL
Olive (or cooking) oil	1 tbsp.	15 mL
Red wine vinegar	2 tsp.	10 mL
Granulated sugar	1/2 tsp.	2 mL
Salt	1/4 tsp.	1 mL
Pepper, just a pinch		
Baguette bread loaf, cut diagonally into 1/2 inch (12 mm) slices (about 30)	1	1
Olive (or cooking) oil	2 tbsp.	30 mL
Garlic clove, halved	1	1
Feta cheese, crumbled (about 1 cup, 250 mL)	4 1/2 oz.	125 g

Preheat gas barbecue to high. Cook peppers on greased grill for 10 to 15 minutes until skins are blackened and blistered. Place in bowl or resealable freezer bag. Cover or seal. Let stand for 10 minutes. Peel and discard skins. Chop peppers finely. Put into medium bowl.

Add next 7 ingredients. Stir. Cover. Chill for 1 hour. Makes 1 cup (250 mL) pepper mixture.

Brush both sides of each baguette slice with second amount of olive oil. Toast on both sides on grill over low heat.

Rub 1 side of each slice with garlic. Divide pepper mixture over garlic sides.

Sprinkle with feta cheese. Makes about 30 bruschetta.

1 bruschetta: 48 Calories; 2.5 g Total Fat (1.3 g Mono, 0.2 g Poly, 0.9 g Sat); 4 mg Cholesterol; 5 g Carbohydrate; trace Fibre; 1 g Protein; 114 mg Sodium

Pictured on page 17.

Eggplant And Goat Cheese Stacks

Layers of eggplant, tomato and goat cheese sandwiched together and drizzled with pesto. Serve with thick slices of toasted bread.

Small eggplant, cut into 8 slices (1/4 inch, 6 mm, thick)	1	1
Olive (or cooking) oil	1 1/2 tbsp.	25 mL
Roma (plum) tomatoes, cut into thirds lengthwise	4	4
Olive (or cooking) oil	2 tsp.	10 mL
Salt	1/2 tsp.	2 mL
Goat cheese, crumbled (about 2/3 cup, 150 mL)	4 oz.	113 g
PESTO SAUCE		
Basil pesto	3 tbsp.	50 mL
Sweet (or regular) chili sauce	2 tbsp.	30 mL
Olive (or cooking) oil	2 1/2 tbsp.	37 mL
Balsamic vinegar	1 tbsp.	15 mL

Brush both sides of each slice of eggplant with first amount of olive oil. Preheat electric grill for 5 minutes or gas barbecue to medium. Cook eggplant on greased grill for about 3 minutes per side until soft and browned.

Brush tomato wedges with second amount of olive oil. Sprinkle with salt. Cook on greased grill for 2 to 3 minutes per side until grill marks appear.

Place 1 slice of eggplant on each of 4 serving plates. Top each with 3 tomato wedges. Divide and sprinkle goat cheese over tomato wedges. Top with remaining eggplant slices.

Pesto Sauce: Put all 4 ingredients into small bowl. Stir until well combined. Makes about 1/2 cup (125 mL) sauce. Drizzle 2 tbsp. (30 mL) sauce over each eggplant stack. Serves 4.

1 serving: 340 Calories; 28.5 g Total Fat (16.3 g Mono, 2.1 g Poly, 8.6 g Sat); 22 mg Cholesterol; 16 g Carbohydrate; 2 g Fibre; 9 g Protein; 573 mg Sodium

On-The-Deck Crostini

Roasted garlic and tomato flavours on crisp baguette slices.
Slight tang from balsamic vinegar is so delicious with tomatoes.

Large garlic bulb, top trimmed to expose cloves	1	1
Olive (or cooking) oil	2 tsp.	10 mL
Large roma (plum) tomatoes, halved lengthwise	8	8
Olive (or cooking) oil	2 tbsp.	30 mL
Balsamic vinegar	1 tbsp.	15 mL
Salt	1/2 tsp.	2 mL
Pepper, sprinkle		
Baguette bread loaf, cut diagonally into 3/4 inch (2 cm) slices (about 28)	1	1
Olive (or cooking) oil	2 tbsp.	30 mL

Drizzle garlic bulb with first amount of olive oil. Preheat gas barbecue to medium. Place garlic bulb on warming rack of barbecue. Close lid. Cook for about 25 minutes until soft. Remove to plate to cool. Squeeze garlic from cloves into small dish. Mash with fork.

Coat tomatoes with second amount of olive oil in large bowl. Place, skin-side down, on ungreased grill for about 5 minutes until skin is loosened and dark grill marks appear. Turn. Cook for about 5 minutes until soft. Remove to cutting board. Cool slightly. Remove and discard skin and most seeds. Chop coarsely. Drain excess juices. Place in medium bowl. Mash with fork. Add garlic.

Stir in vinegar, salt and pepper. Makes 2 cups (500 mL) tomato mixture.

Brush both sides of each baguette slice with third amount of olive oil. Toast on both sides on grill over low heat. Spread with tomato mixture to serve or provide small spreading knives. Makes about 28 crostini.

1 crostini: 52 Calories; 2.7 g Total Fat (1.8 g Mono, 0.3 g Poly, 0.4 g Sat); 0 mg Cholesterol; 6 g Carbohydrate; 1 g Fibre; 1 g Protein; 95 mg Sodium

Shrimp And Artichoke Skewers

A beautiful and delicious combination of colours and shapes.

MARINADE

Prepared orange juice	1/2 cup	125 mL
Sherry (or alcohol-free sherry)	1/4 cup	60 mL
Chopped fresh parsley (or 1 tbsp., 15 mL, flakes)	1/4 cup	60 mL
Olive (or cooking) oil	3 tbsp.	50 mL
Grainy mustard	2 tbsp.	30 mL
Maple (or maple-flavoured) syrup	1 1/2 tbsp.	25 mL
Garlic cloves, minced (or 1/2 tsp., 2 mL, powder)	2	2
Salt	1/4 tsp.	1 mL
Raw large shrimp, tails intact (about 30), peeled and deveined	11 oz.	310 g
Can of artichoke hearts, drained and quartered	14 oz.	398 mL
Bamboo skewers (8 inch, 20 cm, length), soaked in water for 10 minutes	10	10

Marinade: Combine first 8 ingredients in jar with tight-fitting lid. Shake well. Pour into medium saucepan. Bring to a boil on medium-high. Boil for 5 to 10 minutes until thickened. Cool. Makes 1 1/4 cups (300 mL) marinade.

Put shrimp into large bowl or resealable freezer bag. Add marinade. Stir to coat. Cover or seal. Marinate in refrigerator for 1 to 3 hours. Thread shrimp and artichoke alternately onto skewers. Brush with any excess marinade. Preheat electric grill for 5 minutes or gas barbecue to medium. Cook skewers on greased grill for about 5 minutes, turning occasionally, until shrimp are pink. Makes 10 skewers.

1 skewer: 92 Calories; 4.7 g Total Fat (3.1 g Mono, 0.6 g Poly, 0.7 g Sat); 32 mg Cholesterol; 7 g Carbohydrate; 1 g Fibre; 5 g Protein; 204 mg Sodium

Pictured on page 17.

Garlic Butter Shrimp

Set the foil pan on a trivet right on the picnic table, provide bread for sopping up the liquid and you'll have the perfect starter for four good friends. Delicious!

Butter (or hard margarine)	3 tbsp.	50 mL
Garlic cloves, minced (or 1/2 tsp., 2 mL, powder)	2	2
Finely chopped shallots (or green onion)	2 tbsp.	30 mL
Cayenne pepper	1/8 tsp.	0.5 mL
Raw medium shrimp, peeled, deveined and with or without tails left intact	1 lb.	454 g
Diced fresh mushrooms	1/4 cup	60 mL
Finely diced red pepper	2 tbsp.	30 mL
Lemon pepper, sprinkle		

Preheat gas barbecue to medium-high. Place shallow foil pan on grill. Add butter. Heat until sizzling and melted, being careful not to brown. Stir in garlic, shallots and cayenne pepper. Cook for 1 to 2 minutes until shallots are soft.

Add shrimp, mushrooms and red pepper. Sprinkle with lemon pepper. Stir. Close lid. Cook for 5 to 6 minutes until shrimp are pink and curled. Serves 4.

1 serving: 176 Calories; 10.3 g Total Fat (2.8 g Mono, 0.9 g Poly, 5.7 g Sat); 153 mg Cholesterol; 3 g Carbohydrate; trace Fibre; 18 g Protein; 216 mg Sodium

1. Shrimp And Artichoke Skewers, page 15
2. Bulgogi Vegetable Bundles, page 22
3. Red Pepper Bruschetta, page 12
4. Grilled Bacon Bites, page 20

Props Courtesy Of: Linens 'N Things

Appetizers

Jumbo Garlic Shrimp

So delicious you'll only want to prepare shrimp on the barbecue from now on.

Hard margarine (or butter)	3 tbsp.	50 mL
Garlic cloves, minced (or 1/2 tsp., 2 mL, powder)	2	2
Grainy mustard	1 1/2 tbsp.	25 mL
Liquid honey	1 1/2 tbsp.	25 mL
Chopped fresh parsley (or 1 1/4 tsp., 6 mL, flakes)	1 1/2 tbsp.	25 mL
Chili paste (sambal oelek)	1/2 tsp.	2 mL
Salt	1/8 tsp.	0.5 mL
Raw jumbo shrimp, peeled, deveined and tails left intact	12	12

Melt margarine in medium saucepan on medium-low. Add garlic. Heat and stir for 2 to 3 minutes until garlic is soft. Remove from heat.

Add next 5 ingredients. Stir.

Cut shrimp down back almost through to other side to butterfly. Preheat gas barbecue to medium. Brush shrimp liberally with margarine mixture. Spread open on greased grill. Cook for about 5 minutes, brushing occasionally with margarine mixture, until shrimp are pink and curled. Makes 12 shrimp.

1 shrimp: 52 Calories; 3.3 g Total Fat (2 g Mono, 0.5 g Poly, 0.7 g Sat); 21 mg Cholesterol; 3 g Carbohydrate; trace Fibre; 3 g Protein; 107 mg Sodium

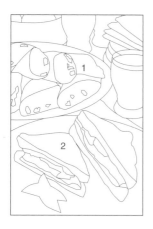

1. Chicken Salsa Wraps, page 31
2. Apple And Cheese Grill, page 37

Props Courtesy Of: Anchor Hocking Canada
Pier 1 Imports

Grilled Bacon Bites

Make these ahead and have them frozen, ready to grill.
Smoky, crisp-cooked bacon envelops a tangy crab morsel.

Chopped imitation (or cooked) crabmeat	1 cup	250 mL
Large egg, fork-beaten	1	1
Seafood cocktail sauce	1/4 cup	60 mL
Soda cracker crumbs	1/2 cup	125 mL
Finely sliced green onion	2 tbsp.	30 mL
Lemon juice	2 tsp.	10 mL
Worcestershire sauce	1/4 tsp.	1 mL
Pickled peppers, minced (optional)	1 tsp.	5 mL
Bacon slices, halved crosswise	11 – 12	11 – 12

Combine first 8 ingredients in medium bowl until moistened. Form into 1 inch (2.5 cm) balls, using 1 tbsp. (15 mL) for each.

Partially cook bacon in large non-stick frying pan on medium for 3 to 4 minutes, turning once or twice, until just starting to brown. Drain on paper towels. Cool. Wrap bacon around crab balls. Secure with wooden picks. Freeze in single layer on baking sheet until firm. Store in freezer bags once frozen. Preheat electric grill for 5 minutes or gas barbecue to medium. Cook frozen crab bites on greased grill for 15 to 20 minutes, turning several times, until bacon is crisp and browned. Remove to paper towels to drain. Serve warm. Makes about 24 appetizers.

1 appetizer: 37 Calories; 1.9 g Total Fat (0.9 g Mono, 0.3 g Poly, 0.6 g Sat); 13 mg Cholesterol; 3 g Carbohydrate; trace Fibre; 2 g Protein; 168 mg Sodium

Pictured on page 17.

Paré Pointer

Bloodhounds are in the money; they are always picking up

Appetizers

Pineapple Chicken Pizzas

Crispy and tangy pizzas on pita breads.

Teriyaki sauce	1/4 cup	60 mL
Brown sugar, packed	1 tsp.	5 mL
Chili sauce	1/2 tsp.	2 mL
Boneless, skinless chicken breast halves (about 2)	8 oz.	225 g
Satay sauce	2 tbsp.	30 mL
Chili sauce	2 tbsp.	30 mL
Small pita breads (3 inch, 7.5 cm, diameter)	12	12
Finely chopped fresh (or canned, drained) pineapple	1/2 cup	125 mL
Finely chopped green pepper	1/3 cup	75 mL
Grated mozzarella cheese	1 cup	250 mL

Combine first 3 ingredients in medium bowl or resealable freezer bag.

Add chicken. Turn to coat. Cover or seal. Marinate in refrigerator for 1 to 3 hours. Drain and discard marinade. Preheat gas barbecue to medium. Cook chicken on greased grill for about 5 minutes per side until no longer pink inside. Finely chop chicken.

Combine satay sauce and second amount of chili sauce in small bowl. Brush 1 side of pitas with satay mixture.

Divide and scatter chicken, pineapple and green pepper over satay mixture. Sprinkle with mozzarella cheese. Place pizzas on greased grill. Close lid. Cook for 3 to 5 minutes until cheese is melted and pitas are crispy. Makes 12 pizzas.

1 pizza: 109 Calories; 3.2 g Total Fat (1 g Mono, 0.4 g Poly, 1.6 g Sat); 19 mg Cholesterol; 12 g Carbohydrate; 1 g Fibre; 8 g Protein; 318 mg Sodium

 tip To allow the smoke to envelop the food and to keep the heat constant, keep the lid of your barbecue closed whenever possible.

Bulgogi Vegetable Bundles

Bulgogi is a popular Korean beef.
This is a great appetizer for a summer patio party.

BULGOGI MARINADE

Water	1/4 cup	60 mL
Indonesian sweet (or thick) soy sauce	1/4 cup	60 mL
Cooking oil	1 tbsp.	15 mL
Sherry (or alcohol-free sherry)	1 tbsp.	15 mL
Garlic cloves (or 1/2 tsp., 2 mL, powder)	2	2
Green onion, cut into 4 pieces	1	1
Sesame seeds, toasted (see Tip, page 146)	2 tsp.	10 mL
Flank steak, cut on the diagonal in 1/8 inch (3 mm) slices	3/4 lb.	340 g
Steamed whole carrots, cut into 4 inch (10 cm) lengths and halved or quartered lengthwise	4	4
Steamed fresh asparagus spears (or whole green beans), cut into 4 inch (10 cm) lengths	10	10
Roasted red peppers, cut into 4 inch (10 cm) strips	2	2
Lightly steamed medium zucchini, cut lengthwise into 8 pieces, cut each into 4 inch (10 cm) lengths	1	1
Bamboo skewers (8 inch, 20 cm, length), soaked in water for 10 minutes	20	20

Bulgogi Marinade: Process first 7 ingredients in blender until smooth. Pour into shallow dish or resealable freezer bag.

Add beef strips. Turn to coat. Cover or seal. Marinate in refrigerator for at least 2 hours or overnight, stirring once or twice. Drain and discard marinade.

(continued on next page)

Divide and layer vegetables among beef strips. Roll up. Thread 2 bundles onto 2 skewers, ladder-style. Repeat with remaining bundles and skewers. Preheat electric grill for 5 minutes or gas barbecue to medium. Cook bundles on greased grill for about 2 1/2 minutes per side until beef is cooked to desired doneness. Makes 20 bundles.

1 bundle: 48 Calories; 1.8 g Total Fat (0.8 g Mono, 0.2 g Poly, 0.6 g Sat); 7 mg Cholesterol; 3 g Carbohydrate; 1 g Fibre; 5 g Protein; 114 mg Sodium

Pictured on page 17.

Mini Chicken Burgers

Easy to make and delicious to eat.

Lean ground chicken	3/4 lb.	340 g
Large egg	1	1
Fine dry bread crumbs	2/3 cup	150 mL
Mango chutney	2 tbsp.	30 mL
Garlic salt	1/2 tsp.	2 mL
Small round dinner rolls, cut in half (buttered, optional)	10	10
Honey mustard	2 tbsp.	30 mL
Sour cream	1/2 cup	125 mL
Swiss cheese, cut into 10 slices	3 oz.	85 g
Mixed baby salad greens	1 – 1 1/2 cups	250 – 375 mL

Combine first 5 ingredients in large bowl. Shape into 10 patties, using 3 tbsp. (50 mL) for each. Heat electric grill for 5 minutes or gas barbecue to medium. Cook patties on greased grill for about 4 minutes per side until no longer pink inside.

Toast cut sides of rolls on grill.

Combine mustard and sour cream in small cup. Divide and spread on toasted sides of rolls. Place patties on bottom halves of rolls.

Divide and top each patty with cheese slice and salad greens. Cover with top halves of rolls. Makes 10 burgers.

1 burger: 218 Calories; 7.6 g Total Fat (2.7 g Mono, 1 g Poly, 3.2 g Sat); 56 mg Cholesterol; 24 g Carbohydrate; 1 g Fibre; 14 g Protein; 430 mg Sodium

Indian Naan Bread

Much like a thick pita in appearance, this bread is excellent when served
with Kefta Wraps, page 74, or Smoked Eggplant Dip, page 110.
Best served warm for a softer texture.

Warm water	1 cup	250 mL
Granulated sugar	2 tsp.	10 mL
Active dry yeast (or 1/4 oz., 8 g, envelope)	1 tbsp.	15 mL
Milk	3 tbsp.	50 mL
Large egg, fork-beaten	1	1
All-purpose flour	4 1/4 cups	1 L
Salt	2 tsp.	10 mL
Hard margarine (or butter), melted	1/4 cup	60 mL

Stir warm water and sugar in small bowl until sugar is dissolved. Sprinkle yeast over top. Let stand for 10 minutes. Stir to dissolve yeast.

Add milk and egg. Stir.

Combine flour and salt in large bowl. Add yeast mixture. Mix until soft dough forms. Knead for about 10 minutes on lightly floured surface until smooth. Place dough in large greased bowl, turning once to grease top. Cover with greased waxed paper and tea towel. Let stand in oven with light on and door closed for about 1 hour until doubled in bulk.

Punch dough down. Knead for 1 to 2 minutes until smooth. Divide and shape into 12 balls. Arrange in single layer on greased baking sheet. Cover with greased waxed paper. Let stand in oven with light on and door closed for about 30 minutes until doubled in size. Quickly roll out 4 dough balls on lightly floured surface to 8 inch (20 cm) diameter circles. Brush both sides with margarine. Repeat with next 4 and then remaining 4. Preheat gas barbecue to medium-high. Carefully place circles on greased grill. Close lid. Cook for about 2 minutes per side until grill marks appear and bread is cooked. Makes 12 breads.

1 bread: 230 Calories; 5 g Total Fat (2.9 g Mono, 0.7 g Poly, 1.1 g Sat); 18 mg Cholesterol; 39 g Carbohydrate; 2 g Fibre; 6 g Protein; 452 mg Sodium

Pictured on page 89.

Tomato-Topped Flatbread

Crispy pita bread topped with ricotta cheese, tomatoes and fresh sweet basil.
A yummy addition to any barbecue!

Olive (or cooking) oil	2 tbsp.	30 mL
Garlic cloves, minced (or 1/2 tsp., 2 mL, powder)	2	2
Large pita breads (8 inch, 20 cm, diameter)	6	6
Ricotta cheese	2 cups	500 mL
Finely chopped roma (plum) tomato	2 1/3 cups	575 mL
Salt, sprinkle		
Pepper, sprinkle		
Finely grated fresh Parmesan cheese	1 cup	250 mL
Coarsely chopped fresh sweet basil (or 1 1/2 tsp., 7 mL, dried)	2 tbsp.	30 mL
Balsamic vinegar	1 tbsp.	15 mL

Combine olive oil and garlic in small bowl. Brush both sides of each pita with olive oil mixture. Preheat electric grill for 5 minutes or gas barbecue to medium-low. Toast 1 side of pitas on greased grill for 3 minutes.

Divide and spread toasted side of each pita with ricotta cheese. Scatter tomato over top. Sprinkle with salt, pepper, Parmesan cheese and basil. Place on greased grill. Cook for 3 to 5 minutes until pitas are crispy and ricotta cheese is soft.

Just before serving, drizzle each pita with balsamic vinegar. Makes 6 breads.

1 bread: 517 Calories; 22.3 g Total Fat (8.2 g Mono, 1.4 g Poly, 11.3 g Sat); 58 mg Cholesterol; 53 g Carbohydrate; 2 g Fibre; 25 g Protein; 861 mg Sodium

Chili Herb Bread

A crisp outer crust with a tender, golden interior. The oregano flavour goes very well with the salty Cheddar cheese and spicy chili undertones. Best served warm.

Hard margarine (or butter), softened	2/3 cup	150 mL
Dried whole oregano	3/4 tsp.	4 mL
Chili powder	1 tsp.	5 mL
Finely grated sharp Cheddar cheese	2/3 cup	150 mL
French bread loaf, cut into 1 inch (2.5 cm) slices	1	1

Mix first 4 ingredients in small bowl.

Divide and spread margarine mixture thickly on 1 side of each bread slice, right to crust edges. Reshape into loaf. Wrap in heavy-duty (or double layer of regular) foil. Preheat gas barbecue to medium. Place loaf on ungreased grill. Close lid. Heat for about 15 minutes, turning occasionally, until heated through. Makes about 14 slices.

1 slice: 195 Calories; 12.1 g Total Fat (6.9 g Mono, 1.2 g Poly, 3.3 g Sat); 6 mg Cholesterol; 17 g Carbohydrate; 1 g Fibre; 4 g Protein; 343 mg Sodium

Pictured on page 35.

Garlic Cheese Bread

A long French bread loaf smothered in a cheesy garlic topping. Great served with barbecued steak and salad.

Grated medium Cheddar cheese	1/2 cup	125 mL
Mayonnaise (not salad dressing)	2/3 cup	150 mL
Finely grated fresh Parmesan cheese	2/3 cup	150 mL
Garlic cloves, minced (or 1/2 tsp., 2 mL, powder)	2	2
Paprika	1/2 tsp.	2 mL
French bread loaf, cut in half horizontally	1	1

(continued on next page)

Combine first 5 ingredients in medium bowl.

Preheat electric grill for 5 minutes or gas barbecue to medium. Toast bread, cut side down, on greased grill for 3 minutes. Divide and spread mayonnaise mixture on toasted sides. Heat, mayonnaise-side up, on greased grill for about 3 minutes until bread is crispy and cheese is melted. Each half cuts into 8 slices, for a total of 16 slices.

1 slice: 185 Calories; 11.2 g Total Fat (5.4 g Mono, 2.9 g Poly, 2.6 g Sat); 13 mg Cholesterol; 15 g Carbohydrate; 1 g Fibre; 5 g Protein; 329 mg Sodium

Chili Cheese Tortillas

Crispy, creamy tortillas that are great on their own or as an appetizer with a meal.

Block of cream cheese, softened	8 oz.	250 g
Sweet (or regular) chili sauce	3 tbsp.	50 mL
Lime juice	2 tbsp.	30 mL
Chopped fresh parsley (or 1 1/2 tsp., 7 mL, flakes)	2 tbsp.	30 mL
Garlic clove, minced (or 1/4 tsp., 1 mL, powder)	1	1
Large flour tortillas (10 inch, 25 cm, diameter)	8	8

Combine first 5 ingredients in medium bowl.

Divide and spread cream cheese mixture liberally on 1 side of tortillas. Preheat electric grill for 5 minutes or gas barbecue to medium. Cook tortillas, cheese-side up, on greased grill for about 5 minutes until bottoms are lightly browned and crispy. Each tortilla cuts into 8 wedges, for a total of 64 wedges.

1 wedge: 39 Calories; 1.9 g Total Fat (0.6 g Mono, 0.3 g Poly, 0.9 g Sat); 4 mg Cholesterol; 5 g Carbohydrate; trace Fibre; 1 g Protein; 58 mg Sodium

Chicken Cheese Burgers

Slightly sweet, well-seasoned patties are topped with fresh, colourful ingredients.

CHICKEN PATTIES

Ground chicken	3/4 lb.	340 g
Fine dry bread crumbs	3/4 cup	175 mL
Finely chopped green onion	1/3 cup	75 mL
Garlic cloves, minced (or 1/2 tsp., 2 mL, powder)	2	2
Large egg, fork-beaten	1	1
Dry onion soup mix, stirred before measuring	2 tbsp.	30 mL
Grainy mustard	2 tbsp.	30 mL
Pepper	1/4 tsp.	1 mL
Cream cheese, softened	1/2 cup	125 mL
Sesame seed buns, cut in half and toasted	4	4
Shredded romaine lettuce	1 cup	250 mL
Whole cranberry sauce	1/4 cup	60 mL

Chicken Patties: Combine first 8 ingredients in large bowl. Divide and shape into 4 patties about 4 inches (10 cm) in diameter. Preheat electric grill for 5 minutes or gas barbecue to medium. Cook patties on greased grill for about 5 minutes per side until no longer pink inside.

Spread cream cheese on bottom half of each bun. Layer with patties and lettuce. Spread cranberry sauce on top half of each bun. Place on top of lettuce. Makes 4 burgers.

1 burger: 540 Calories; 19.3 g Total Fat (5.7 g Mono, 3 g Poly, 8.6 g Sat); 147 mg Cholesterol; 59 g Carbohydrate; 2 g Fibre; 32 g Protein; 1273 mg Sodium

tip　*To ensure that patties made with ground beef are cooked thoroughly, mix and form the patties and then poke your finger through the centre of each to make a "doughnut." As the patties cook, the hole will slowly close, a good visual indicator that the meat in the centre is cooked.*

Peppered Buffalo Burgers

Lean, tender patties are complemented by the
flavours of blue cheese and mushrooms.

BUFFALO PATTIES

Ground buffalo	3/4 lb.	340 g
Finely chopped onion	1/2 cup	125 mL
Fresh fine bread crumbs	1/2 cup	125 mL
Salt	1/4 tsp.	1 mL
Barbecue sauce	2 tbsp.	30 mL
Coarsely ground pepper (or 1 1/2 tsp., 7 mL, regular pepper)	1 tbsp.	15 mL
Fresh medium mushrooms, thinly sliced	14	14
Cooking oil	2 tsp.	10 mL
Salt, sprinkle		
Hamburger buns, cut in half	4	4

BLUE CHEESE SAUCE

Blue cheese, chopped	2 1/2 oz.	70 g
Sour cream	1/4 cup	60 mL

Buffalo Patties: Combine first 5 ingredients in large bowl. Divide and shape into 4 patties about 3 1/2 inches (9 cm) in diameter.

Divide and sprinkle with pepper. Preheat electric grill for 5 minutes or gas barbecue to medium-high. Cook patties on well-greased grill for about 5 minutes per side until no longer pink inside.

Combine mushrooms, cooking oil and salt in medium bowl. Cook directly on greased electric grill or in foil pan on barbecue grill for about 5 minutes, turning occasionally, until lightly browned.

Toast cut sides of buns on grill.

Blue Cheese Sauce: Combine blue cheese and sour cream in small saucepan. Heat and stir on medium for about 3 minutes until cheese is melted. Makes 1/2 cup (125 mL) sauce. Divide and spread on toasted sides of each bun. Layer patty and mushrooms on bottom half of each bun. Cover with top half of each bun. Makes 4 burgers.

1 burger: 407 Calories; 14.5 g Total Fat (5.3 g Mono, 2 g Poly, 6.2 g Sat); 59 mg Cholesterol; 40 g Carbohydrate; 2 g Fibre; 29 g Protein; 894 mg Sodium

Lentil Burgers

These healthy patties are flavoured with warm spices and curry.

LENTIL PATTIES		
Chopped potato	1 1/2 cups	375 mL
Chopped yam	1 cup	250 mL
Water		
Salt	1/4 tsp.	1 mL
Can of green lentils, rinsed and drained	19 oz.	540 mL
Large egg, fork-beaten	1	1
Ground almonds	1/3 – 1/2 cup	75 – 125 mL
Ground cinnamon	1/4 tsp.	1 mL
Chopped fresh parsley (or 1 tbsp., 15 mL, flakes)	1/4 cup	60 mL
Chopped green onion	1/4 cup	60 mL
Mild curry paste	2 tbsp.	30 mL
Granulated sugar	1 tsp.	5 mL
Cooking oil	1 tbsp.	15 mL
Crusty round buns, cut in half	6	6
Sour cream	1/3 cup	75 mL
Sweet (or regular) chili sauce	3 tbsp.	50 mL
English cucumber, with peel, thinly sliced	1/4	1/4

Lentil Patties: Cook potato and yam in water and salt in medium saucepan for about 10 minutes until tender. Drain well.

Combine next 8 ingredients in large bowl. Add potato and yam. Stir. Put 1/2 of mixture into food processor. Process until well mixed. Return to remaining lentil mixture. Mix well. Shape into patties, using 2/3 cup (150 mL) for each.

Brush both sides of each patty with cooking oil. Preheat electric grill for 5 minutes or gas barbecue to medium. Cook patties on well-greased grill for about 7 minutes per side until golden.

Toast cut sides of buns on grill.

Combine sour cream and chili sauce in small bowl. Divide and spread on toasted sides of each bun.

Layer patty and cucumber on bottom half of each bun. Cover with top halves. Makes 6 burgers.

1 burger: 394 Calories; 11.5 g Total Fat (5.1 g Mono, 2.8 g Poly, 2.3 g Sat); 41 mg Cholesterol; 60 g Carbohydrate; 4 g Fibre; 14 g Protein; 563 mg Sodium

Burgers & More

Chicken Salsa Wraps

Satisfying, crispy wraps with a tender chicken filling.

Salsa	1/2 cup	125 mL
Lime juice	3 tbsp.	50 mL
Ground cumin	1 tsp.	5 mL
Granulated sugar	1 tsp.	5 mL
Boneless, skinless chicken breast halves (about 4)	1 lb.	454 g
Cooking oil	1 tbsp.	15 mL
Large red pepper, quartered	1	1
Fresh medium mushrooms, sliced	16	16
Sour cream	1/3 cup	75 mL
Salsa	1/4 cup	60 mL
Jalapeño tortillas (or your choice)	4	4
Grated Monterey Jack With Jalapeño cheese	1 cup	250 mL
Ripe large avocado, sliced	1	1
Hard margarine (or butter), melted	1 – 2 tbsp.	15 – 30 mL

Combine first 4 ingredients in shallow dish or resealable freezer bag.

Add chicken. Turn to coat. Cover or seal. Marinate in refrigerator for at least 3 hours or overnight. Drain and discard marinade. Preheat electric grill for 5 minutes or gas barbecue to medium. Cook chicken on well-greased grill for about 5 minutes per side until no longer pink inside. Cut into 1/8 inch (3 mm) thick slices.

Combine cooking oil, red pepper and mushrooms in medium bowl. Cook directly on greased electric grill or in foil pan on barbecue grill for about 10 minutes, turning occasionally, until pepper is tender-crisp and mushrooms are browned.

Combine sour cream and second amount of salsa in small bowl. Divide and spread over each tortilla.

Sprinkle with cheese. Divide and layer avocado, chicken, red pepper and mushrooms down centre of each tortilla. Roll up to enclose filling. Brush with margarine. Cook wraps on greased grill for about 2 minutes, turning occasionally, until crisp and golden. Makes 4 wraps.

1 wrap: 666 Calories; 32.9 g Total Fat (14.7 g Mono, 5 g Poly, 10.9 g Sat); 124 mg Cholesterol; 47 g Carbohydrate; 5 g Fibre; 47 g Protein; 588 mg Sodium

Pictured on page 18.

Bacon-Wrapped Dogs

The crispy bacon and tangy mustard make these delicious!

Bacon slices	8	8
Prepared mustard	4 tsp.	20 mL
Wieners	8	8
Hot dog buns (buttered, optional)	8	8

Spread 1 side of each bacon slice with 1/2 tsp. (2 mL) mustard. Wrap bacon, mustard-side in, diagonally around wieners. Secure ends with wooden picks. Preheat electric grill for 5 minutes or gas barbecue to medium. Arrange wieners on greased grill. Cook for about 30 minutes, turning frequently, until bacon is crisp.

Insert wrapped wieners into buns. Makes 8 hot dogs.

1 hot dog: *271 Calories; 14.2 g Total Fat (6.8 g Mono, 1.6 g Poly, 4.9 g Sat); 24 mg Cholesterol; 24 g Carbohydrate; trace Fibre; 10 g Protein; 754 mg Sodium*

Dressy Dogs

A sweet, sticky sauce coats ordinary wieners making them special.

Apricot jam	1/2 cup	125 mL
Apple cider vinegar	3 tbsp.	50 mL
Brown sugar, packed	1 tbsp.	15 mL
Soy sauce	1 tbsp.	15 mL
Prepared mustard	1 tsp.	5 mL
Wieners	12	12
Hot dog buns	12	12

Stir first 5 ingredients in small saucepan on low until brown sugar is dissolved.

Score each wiener diagonally or crosswise. Preheat electric grill for 5 minutes or gas barbecue to medium. Cook wieners on greased grill for about 10 minutes, turning and brushing with sauce often, until browned.

Serve wieners in buns. Makes 12 hot dogs.

1 hot dog: *272 Calories; 11 g Total Fat (5.2 g Mono, 1.2 g Poly, 3.8 g Sat); 19 mg Cholesterol; 34 g Carbohydrate; trace Fibre; 8 g Protein; 714 mg Sodium*

Burgers & More

Tomato Chickpea Patties

These attractive, mildly-flavoured patties go well with this colourful salsa.
Serve on their own or topped with condiments in a bun.

Cans of chickpeas (19 oz., 540 mL, each), rinsed and drained	2	2
Large egg	1	1
Fine dry bread crumbs	1/2 cup	125 mL
Sun-dried tomato pesto	1/3 cup	75 mL
Chopped fresh parsley (or 1 tbsp., 15 mL, flakes)	1/4 cup	60 mL
Olive (or cooking) oil	1 tbsp.	15 mL
ZUCCHINI PEACH SALSA		
Medium zucchini, sliced lengthwise, 1/4 inch (6 mm) thick	1	1
Medium red pepper, quartered	1	1
Can of peach halves, drained and finely chopped	14 oz.	398 mL
White wine vinegar	1 tbsp.	15 mL
Olive (or cooking) oil	1 tbsp.	15 mL
Garlic clove, minced (or 1/4 tsp., 1 mL, powder)	1	1
Salt, just a pinch		
Pepper, just a pinch		

Put first 5 ingredients into food processor. Process until well combined and chickpeas are finely chopped. Shape into eight 4 inch (10 cm) patties, using 1/2 cup (125 mL) for each.

Preheat electric grill for 5 minutes or gas barbecue to medium-high. Brush both sides of each patty with olive oil. Cook patties on greased grill for about 5 minutes per side until browned. Makes 8 patties.

Zucchini Peach Salsa: Cook zucchini and red pepper on grill for about 5 minutes per side until browned. Chop finely. Put into medium bowl.

Add remaining 6 ingredients. Stir. Makes 2 cups (500 mL) salsa. Serve with patties. Serves 4.

1 serving: 395 Calories; 13.5 g Total Fat (7.4 g Mono, 2.6 g Poly, 2 g Sat); 54 mg Cholesterol; 56 g Carbohydrate; 8 g Fibre; 16 g Protein; 459 mg Sodium

Mushroom Patties

A veggie patty with a wonderful texture and a delicious mushroom flavour.
Serve as is or pile with condiments in a bun.

Large eggs	2	2
Dried whole oregano	1 tsp.	5 mL
Dried sweet basil	1 tsp.	5 mL
Garlic salt	1 1/2 tsp.	7 mL
Pepper	1/2 tsp.	2 mL
Whole wheat (or regular) soda cracker crumbs	2/3 cup	150 mL
Green onions, sliced	2	2
Finely chopped fresh mushrooms	2 cups	500 mL
Crumbled shredded wheat cereal biscuits	1 cup	250 mL
Grated sharp Cheddar cheese	1 cup	250 mL

Mix first 5 ingredients in medium bowl.

Add cracker crumbs and green onion. Mix.

Add mushrooms, shredded wheat and cheese. Stir until well moistened.
Divide and shape into 4 patties about 3 1/2 inches (9 cm) in diameter.
Preheat electric grill for 5 minutes or gas barbecue to medium. Cook
patties on greased grill for 15 minutes. Turn carefully. Cook for about
5 minutes until firm and browned. Makes 4 patties.

*1 patty: 335 Calories; 16 g Total Fat (5.3 g Mono, 1.2 g Poly, 7.6 g Sat); 139 mg Cholesterol;
35 g Carbohydrate; 6 g Fibre; 16 g Protein; 777 mg Sodium*

1. Chili Herb Bread, page 26
2. Seafood Pasta, page 84

Props Courtesy Of: Casa Bugatti
The Bay

Burgers & More

Apple And Cheese Grill

Tasty grilled sandwiches to serve at any time of the day!
The sweet apple slices add a slight crispness to the otherwise soft filling.

Raisin bread slices (about 3/4 inch, 2 cm, thick)	8	8
Hard margarine (or butter), softened	6 tbsp.	100 mL
Honey mustard	1/4 cup	60 mL
Thin ham slices	12	12
Large cooking apple (such as McIntosh), peeled and thinly sliced (about 1 1/2 cups, 375 mL)	1	1
Grated sharp Cheddar cheese	1 1/2 cups	375 mL

Spread 1 side of each bread slice with margarine. Place 4 bread slices, margarine-side down, on cutting board. Spread with mustard.

Layer with ham, apple and cheese. Place remaining 4 bread slices, margarine-side up, on top of cheese. Preheat electric grill for 5 minutes or gas barbecue to medium. Cook sandwiches on greased grill for about 6 minutes per side until golden and cheese is melted. Makes 4 sandwiches.

1 sandwich: 807 Calories; 47.5 g Total Fat (22.7 g Mono, 4.3 g Poly, 17.6 g Sat); 108 mg Cholesterol; 61 g Carbohydrate; 4 g Fibre; 37 g Protein; 2291 mg Sodium

Pictured on page 18.

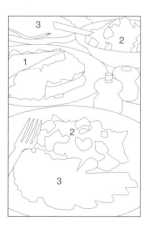

1. Grilled Polenta And Salad, page 130
2. Grilled Ratatouille Salsa, page 100
3. Mustard Seasoned Steak, page 44

Props Courtesy Of: Pfaltzgraff Canada

Roasted Pork Sandwiches

This is an easy recipe but does require some time to make.
The end result, however, is well worth the effort!
Serve with your favourite coleslaw or potato salad.

CHILI RUB		
Brown sugar, packed	1 tbsp.	15 mL
Chili powder	1 tbsp.	15 mL
Dried sage	1 tbsp.	15 mL
Salt	1 tbsp.	15 mL
Coarsely ground pepper (or 1 1/2 tsp., 7 mL, regular pepper)	1 tbsp.	15 mL
Pork shoulder butt roast	4 lbs.	1.8 kg
SAUCE		
Malt vinegar	1/2 cup	125 mL
Applesauce	2/3 cup	150 mL
Brown sugar, packed	1/3 cup	75 mL
White rolls, cut in half	12	12

Chili Rub: Combine first 5 ingredients in small bowl. Measure 1 1/2 tbsp. (25 mL) into medium saucepan. Set saucepan aside.

Put roast into medium bowl. Rub remaining seasoning mixture all over roast. Cover. Let stand in refrigerator for at least 6 hours or up to 24 hours. Remove from refrigerator 30 minutes before cooking. Preheat gas barbecue to high. Turn off centre or left burner. Place roast on greased grill over drip pan on unlit side. Close lid. Reduce heat to low. Cook for about 4 1/2 hours until tender and internal temperature reads 150°F (65°C). Remove roast. Cover completely in foil. Let stand for 30 minutes. Cut into small pieces. Makes about 4 cups (1 L) pork.

Sauce: Add first 3 ingredients to reserved seasoning mixture. Heat and stir on medium-high until brown sugar is dissolved. Bring to a boil. Reduce heat to medium-low. Simmer, uncovered, for about 10 minutes, stirring occasionally, until thickened. Makes about 2/3 cup (150 mL) sauce.

Divide and spread sauce on cut sides of rolls. Divide pork over sauce on bottom halves of rolls. Cover with top halves of rolls. Makes 12 sandwiches.

1 sandwich: 427 Calories; 21.5 g Total Fat (9.5 g Mono, 2.2 g Poly, 7.6 g Sat); 68 mg Cholesterol; 32 g Carbohydrate; trace Fibre; 25 g Protein; 899 mg Sodium

Grilled Quesadillas

Crispy on the outside and a spicy chicken filling on the inside.

Shredded cooked chicken	3 cups	750 mL
Sour cream	1/3 cup	75 mL
Chili sauce	2 tbsp.	30 mL
Grated Monterey Jack cheese	1 2/3 cups	400 mL
Large flour tortillas (10 inch, 25 cm, diameter)	4	4
Sliced pickled jalapeño peppers, drained, chopped	1 – 2 tbsp.	15 – 30 mL
Medium ripe tomatoes, quartered, seeded and diced	2	2
Finely chopped green onion	3 tbsp.	50 mL
Chopped fresh parsley (or 1 1/2 tsp., 7 mL, flakes)	2 tbsp.	30 mL
Cooking oil	1 tbsp.	15 mL

Combine first 3 ingredients in medium bowl.

Divide and sprinkle cheese over 1/2 of each tortilla. Divide and spread chicken mixture over cheese.

Divide and layer next 4 ingredients over chicken mixture. Fold tortillas in half to cover filling.

Brush tops with cooking oil. Preheat electric grill for 5 minutes or gas barbecue to medium. Cook quesadillas, top-side down, on greased grill for 5 minutes. Brush with cooking oil. Turn. Cook for about 5 minutes until crisp and golden and cheese is melted. Cut in half to serve. Makes 4 quesadillas.

1 quesadilla: 681 Calories; 34.2 g Total Fat (12 g Mono, 5.2 g Poly, 14.5 g Sat); 152 mg Cholesterol; 40 g Carbohydrate; 3 g Fibre; 51 g Protein; 808 mg Sodium

tip   *If a flare-up occurs, move the food to one side of the grill until flames die down. Serious flare-ups can be doused with baking soda. Never use water on gas barbecues, except when using wood chips (see Wood Chips & Other Aromatics, page 110).*

Steak Sandwiches

*Juicy steak with a warm garlic butter spread. Add your own
selection of ingredients to the sandwiches if desired.*

GARLIC BUTTER

Butter (or hard margarine), softened	1/4 cup	60 mL
Garlic cloves, minced (or 1/2 tsp., 2 mL, powder)	2	2
Chopped fresh chives (or 2 1/4 tsp., 11 mL, dried)	3 tbsp.	50 mL
Cajun seasoning	2 tsp.	10 mL
French bread slices (about 1/2 inch, 12 mm, thick)	8	8
Fast-fry steaks (about 10 oz., 285 g)	4	4
Portobello mushrooms (about 4 inch, 10 cm, diameter)	4	4
Cooking oil	2 tsp.	10 mL
Salt, just a pinch		
Barbecue sauce	1/4 cup	60 mL
Swiss cheese slices (2 1/2 oz., 70 g)	4	4

Garlic Butter: Combine first 4 ingredients in small bowl. Spread mixture on 1 side of each bread slice.

Preheat electric grill for 5 minutes or gas barbecue to medium-high. Cook steaks on greased grill for 3 to 4 minutes per side until desired doneness. Keep warm.

Combine mushrooms, cooking oil and salt in medium bowl. Cook mushrooms on greased grill, turning occasionally, for about 5 minutes until soft and browned. Slice mushrooms thinly. Keep warm. Toast buttered side of bread slices on greased grill.

Spread toasted side of 4 bread slices with barbecue sauce. Layer with cheese, steak and mushrooms. Top with remaining bread slices, toasted side up. Makes 4 sandwiches.

1 sandwich: 508 Calories; 25.6 g Total Fat (8.7 g Mono, 2.1 g Poly, 12.7 g Sat); 77 mg Cholesterol; 44 g Carbohydrate; 4 g Fibre; 26 g Protein; 1355 mg Sodium

Cajun-Style Marinated Roast

Tender, lean beef with a deep brown coating and just a hint of heat.

CAJUN MARINADE

Paprika	3 tbsp.	50 mL
Coarsely ground pepper (or 1 1/2 tsp., 7 mL, pepper)	1 tbsp.	15 mL
Cayenne pepper	1 tbsp.	15 mL
Dried oregano	1 tbsp.	15 mL
Dried thyme leaves	1 tbsp.	15 mL
Garlic cloves, minced (or 1 1/2 tsp., 7 mL, powder)	6	6
Minced onion	1/4 cup	60 mL
Can of beer	12 1/2 oz.	355 mL
Eye of round beef roast, poked deeply all over with meat fork	3 lbs.	1.4 kg
Seasoned salt	2 tsp.	10 mL

Cajun Marinade: Measure first 5 ingredients into small bowl. Stir. Add garlic, onion and beer. Stir. Makes 2 cups (500 mL) marinade. Pour into resealable freezer bag or container large enough to hold roast.

Add roast. Turn to coat well. Seal or cover. Marinate in refrigerator overnight or for up to 48 hours, turning several times. Drain and discard marinade. Pat roast dry with paper towels.

Sprinkle seasoned salt all over roast. Preheat gas barbecue to high. Turn off centre or left burner. Place roast on greased grill over drip pan on unlit side. Close lid. Cook for 1 1/2 to 2 hours until meat thermometer reads 160°F (75°C) for medium or until desired doneness. Let stand, tented with foil, for 15 minutes before slicing thinly. Serves 12.

1 serving: 179 Calories; 7.9 g Total Fat (3.3 g Mono, 0.4 g Poly, 3.1 g Sat); 49 mg Cholesterol; 2 g Carbohydrate; trace Fibre; 23 g Protein; 245 mg Sodium

Paré Pointer

Most turkeys barely eat. They are always stuffed.

Big Beef Brisket

Long, slow cooking is the ticket to a tender finished product.
This lean, melt-in-your-mouth beef is great on its own or in
sandwiches or wraps for a lunchtime treat.

SPICY SAUCE

Hickory-smoked (or mesquite) barbecue sauce	1 cup	250 mL
Blackstrap molasses	1/4 cup	60 mL
Chili sauce	1/4 cup	60 mL
Worcestershire sauce	3 tbsp.	50 mL
Garlic powder	1/2 tsp.	2 mL
Onion powder	1/2 tsp.	2 mL
Hot pepper sauce	1/2 tsp.	2 mL
Beef brisket, flat (not rolled)	4 lbs.	1.8 kg
Coarsely ground pepper, sprinkle		

Spicy Sauce: Combine first 7 ingredients in small bowl. Makes 1 3/4 cups (425 mL) basting sauce.

Sprinkle brisket on both sides with pepper. Preheat gas barbecue to medium. Turn off centre or left burner. Place brisket on greased grill over drip pan on unlit side. Close lid. Cook for 2 1/2 to 3 hours, turning and brushing liberally with sauce several times, until very tender. Let stand, tented with foil, for at least 15 minutes before cutting across grain on diagonal into 1/4 inch (6 mm) thick slices. Serves 16.

1 serving: 350 Calories; 26.4 g Total Fat (11.6 g Mono, 1.1 g Poly, 10.3 g Sat); 63 mg Cholesterol; 7 g Carbohydrate; 1 g Fibre; 20 g Protein; 283 mg Sodium

Paré Pointer

To make mistakes is one thing but to practise them is another.

Main Dishes

Spicy Stuffed Beef

The mild stuffing inside is complemented by the spicy rub.

RAISIN 'N' BREAD STUFFING		
Fresh coarse bread crumbs	2 cups	500 mL
Chopped raisins	1/2 cup	125 mL
Chopped water chestnuts (1/2 of 8 oz., 227 mL, can)	1/2 cup	125 mL
Chopped green onion	1/4 cup	60 mL
Hard margarine (or butter), melted	3 tbsp.	50 mL
Chopped fresh thyme leaves (or 3/4 tsp., 4 mL, dried)	1 tbsp.	15 mL
Rib-eye roast	2 – 2 1/2 lbs.	900 g – 1.1 kg
ONION HERB RUB		
Brown sugar, packed	2 tbsp.	30 mL
Onion powder	1 tbsp.	15 mL
Paprika	1 tbsp.	15 mL
Garlic powder	2 tsp.	10 mL
Salt	1/2 tsp.	2 mL
Pepper	1/2 tsp.	2 mL

Raisin 'N' Bread Stuffing: Combine first 6 ingredients in medium bowl. Makes 3 cups (750 mL) stuffing.

Cut deep pocket in side of roast almost all the way through to the other side. Spoon stuffing into pocket. Tie roast, at 1 inch (2.5 cm) intervals, with butcher's string.

Onion Herb Rub: Combine all 6 ingredients on sheet of waxed paper. Makes about 1/3 cup (75 mL) rub. Roll roast in herb rub to coat evenly. Preheat gas barbecue to high. Turn off centre or left burner. Place roast on greased grill over drip pan on unlit side. Close lid. Cook for 35 minutes. Turn roast. Cook for 40 to 45 minutes until meat thermometer reads 145°F (63°C) for medium or until desired doneness. Let stand for 15 minutes. Cut into 1/2 inch (12 mm) thick slices. Serves 8.

1 serving: 394 Calories; 15.7 g Total Fat (7.6 g Mono, 1.3 g Poly, 5.2 g Sat); 51 mg Cholesterol; 37 g Carbohydrate; 2 g Fibre; 26 g Protein; 495 mg Sodium

Mustard Seasoned Steak

*Visible mustard seeds make this steak pleasing to look at,
as well as delicious. Slice the steak thinly across the grain
on the diagonal for the best presentation.*

MUSTARD WINE MARINADE

Grainy mustard	1/4 cup	60 mL
White (or alcohol-free) wine	1/4 cup	60 mL
Apple cider vinegar	2 tbsp.	30 mL
Cooking oil	2 tbsp.	30 mL
Finely chopped fresh rosemary (or 3/4 tsp., 4 mL, dried)	1 tbsp.	15 mL
Pepper, sprinkle		
Flank steak (about 1 1/2 lbs., 680 g)	1	1

Mustard Wine Marinade: Combine first 6 ingredients in shallow dish or resealable freezer bag. Makes about 2/3 cup (150 mL) marinade.

Add steak. Turn to coat. Cover or seal. Marinate in refrigerator for at least 6 hours or overnight. Drain, reserving marinade. Pat steak dry with paper towels. Boil marinade in small saucepan for 5 minutes. Preheat electric grill for 5 minutes or gas barbecue to high. Cook steak on greased grill for 2 minutes per side to sear. Cook for 5 to 7 minutes per side, brushing often with marinade, for medium-rare or until desired doneness. Let stand, tented with foil, for 10 minutes. Cut diagonally across the grain into very thin slices to serve. Serves 6.

1 serving: 251 Calories; 14.2 g Total Fat (6.4 g Mono, 2.1 g Poly, 4.2 g Sat); 46 mg Cholesterol; 1 g Carbohydrate; 0 g Fibre; 27 g Protein; 199 mg Sodium

Pictured on page 36.

Paré Pointer

I understand that cooking oil was invented on a fry-day.

Beer 'N' Spice Steak

Dark glazed beef with a slightly sweet cinnamon taste.
Addition of beer will prompt the question, "What is that taste?"

BEER MARINADE

Can of beer	12 1/2 oz.	355 mL
Brown sugar, packed	2 tbsp.	30 mL
Prepared mustard	2 tsp.	10 mL
Garlic powder (optional)	1/4 tsp.	1 mL
Ground cinnamon	1/8 tsp.	0.5 mL
Pepper	1/8 tsp.	0.5 mL
Top sirloin steak (about 1 1/2 lbs., 680 g)	1	1
Cooking oil	1 tbsp.	15 mL
Salt	1/2 tsp.	2 mL
Pepper, sprinkle		

Beer Marinade: Combine first 6 ingredients in shallow dish or resealable freezer bag. Makes about 1 1/2 cups (375 mL) marinade.

Add steak. Turn to coat. Cover or seal. Marinate in refrigerator for at least 6 hours or overnight, turning occasionally. Drain, reserving marinade. Pat steak dry with paper towels. Boil marinade in small saucepan for 5 minutes.

Brush steak with cooking oil. Sprinkle both sides with salt and pepper. Preheat electric grill for 5 minutes or gas barbecue to high. Cook steak on greased grill for 8 to 10 minutes per side, brushing several times with marinade, for medium or until desired doneness. Cut into 6 portions to serve. Serves 6.

1 serving: 213 Calories; 9.8 g Total Fat (4.5 g Mono, 1 g Poly, 3.1 g Sat); 50 mg Cholesterol; 7 g Carbohydrate; trace Fibre; 19 g Protein; 264 mg Sodium

Buttered Steak And Shrimp

Grilled steak topped with a slightly sweet, garlic-flavoured butter and shrimp.

Rib-eye medallions (filet mignon), about 4 oz. (113 g) each	4	4
Cooking oil	1 tbsp.	15 mL
Salt	1/4 tsp.	1 mL
Pepper	1/4 tsp.	1 mL
Raw large shrimp (about 3 oz., 85 g), peeled, deveined and tails left intact	12	12
HONEY MUSTARD BUTTER		
Cooking oil	2 tsp.	10 mL
Finely chopped red onion	2 tbsp.	30 mL
Garlic clove, minced (or 1/4 tsp., 1 mL, powder)	1	1
Butter (or hard margarine), softened	1/3 cup	75 mL
Honey mustard	2 tbsp.	30 mL
Chopped fresh parsley (or 3/4 – 1 1/2 tsp., 4 – 7 mL, flakes)	1 – 2 tbsp.	15 – 30 mL
Pepper	1/4 tsp.	1 mL

Brush both sides of each medallion with cooking oil. Sprinkle with salt and pepper. Preheat gas barbecue to medium-high. Place steaks on greased grill. Cook for about 7 minutes per side for medium or until desired doneness.

Cook shrimp on greased grill on medium-high for about 2 minutes per side until pink and curled. Do not overcook.

Honey Mustard Butter: Heat cooking oil in small saucepan on medium-low. Add red onion and garlic. Cook for about 5 minutes until onion is soft. Put into small bowl. Cool.

Add remaining 4 ingredients. Stir until well combined. Shape mixture into 4 inch (10 cm) log on waxed paper. Wrap. Chill for 1 to 2 hours until firm. Cut into 1/2 inch (12 mm) rounds. Place 2 rounds and 3 shrimp on top of each hot steak. Serves 4.

1 serving: 504 Calories; 36.8 g Total Fat (14.3 g Mono, 3.1 g Poly, 16.3 g Sat); 152 mg Cholesterol; 6 g Carbohydrate; trace Fibre; 37 g Protein; 464 mg Sodium

Pictured on front cover.

Beef Roulade

A ground beef mixture filled with spinach, peaches and pistachios.

Lean ground beef	1 1/2 lbs.	680 g
Large egg, fork-beaten	1	1
Envelope of dry onion soup mix	1 1/4 oz.	38 g
Fine dry bread crumbs	1/2 cup	125 mL
FILLING		
Box of frozen spinach, thawed and squeezed dry	10 oz.	300 g
Can of sliced peaches, drained and finely chopped	14 oz.	398 mL
Pistachios, toasted (see Tip, page 146) and coarsely chopped	1/2 cup	125 mL
GLAZE		
Worcestershire sauce	1 tbsp.	15 mL
Liquid honey, warmed	1 tbsp.	15 mL

Combine first 4 ingredients in large bowl. Place mixture on large piece of waxed paper. Shape into 10 × 12 inch (25 × 30 cm) rectangle with short side at bottom.

Filling: Put spinach into medium bowl. Add peaches and pistachios. Mix well. Spread ground beef mixture with filling to within 1 inch (2.5 cm) of all edges. Using waxed paper as guide, roll up jelly roll-style from short side. Discard waxed paper. Preheat gas barbecue to high. Turn off centre or left burner. Place roulade in greased foil pan on unlit side of grill. Close lid. Cook for 45 minutes.

Glaze: Combine Worcestershire sauce and honey in small bowl. Brush roulade with glaze. Close lid. Cook for 5 to 10 minutes until roulade is browned, glazed and no longer pink inside. Let stand for 15 minutes before cutting into 1 inch (2.5 cm) slices. Cuts into 10 slices.

1 slice: 247 Calories; 14.6 g Total Fat (7.1 g Mono, 1.1 g Poly, 4.8 g Sat); 60 mg Cholesterol; 13 g Carbohydrate; 2 g Fibre; 16 g Protein; 473 mg Sodium

Indonesian Beef Skewers

Served with peanut sauce for dipping.
These tasty skewers would also make a great appetizer.

INDONESIAN MARINADE

Indonesian sweet (or thick) soy sauce	1/4 cup	60 mL
Barbecue sauce (your choice)	3 tbsp.	50 mL
Worcestershire sauce	3 tbsp.	50 mL
Maple (or maple-flavoured) syrup	1/4 cup	60 mL
Chili sauce	2 tbsp.	30 mL
Dijon mustard	2 tbsp.	30 mL
Garlic clove, minced (or 1/4 tsp., 1 mL, powder)	1	1
Salt	1/2 tsp.	2 mL
Rib-eye steak, partially frozen, cut lengthwise into 1/8 inch (3 mm) thick slices	2 lbs.	900 g
Bamboo skewers (8 inch, 20 cm, length), soaked in water for 10 minutes	16	16

PEANUT SAUCE

Peanut (or cooking) oil	2 tsp.	10 mL
Finely chopped red onion	2 tbsp.	30 mL
Garlic clove, minced (or 1/4 tsp., 1 mL, powder)	1	1
Finely grated gingerroot (or 1/8 tsp., 0.5 mL, ground ginger)	1/2 tsp.	2 mL
Crunchy peanut butter	1/2 cup	125 mL
Hot water	1/2 cup	125 mL
Chili sauce	1/4 cup	60 mL
Lemon (or lime) juice	2 tbsp.	30 mL
Brown sugar, packed	1 tbsp.	15 mL

Indonesian Marinade: Combine first 8 ingredients in shallow dish or resealable freezer bag. Makes about 1 cup (250 mL) marinade.

Add beef. Stir to coat. Cover or seal. Marinate in refrigerator for at least 8 hours or overnight. Remove beef. Discard marinade.

(continued on next page)

Main Dishes

Thread beef, accordion-style, onto skewers. Preheat electric grill for 5 minutes or gas barbecue to medium. Cook skewers on lightly greased grill for about 8 minutes, turning several times, until beef is tender.

Peanut Sauce: Heat peanut oil in small saucepan on medium-low. Add red onion, garlic and ginger. Cook for about 5 minutes until onion is soft.

Add remaining 5 ingredients. Heat and stir for about 3 minutes until hot. Makes 1 1/3 cups (325 mL) sauce. Serve with skewers. Makes 16 skewers.

1 skewer with 4 tsp. (20 mL) sauce: 172 Calories; 9.3 g Total Fat (4.1 g Mono, 1.6 g Poly, 2.8 g Sat); 23 mg Cholesterol; 7 g Carbohydrate; 1 g Fibre; 16 g Protein; 348 mg Sodium

---

Caveman Beef Ribs

Use your favourite sauce for these very tender, succulent ribs.
Provide lots of paper napkins for those sticky fingers!

Beef ribs, whole slab (4 – 5 lbs., 1.8 – 2.3 kg)	1	1
Garlic powder, sprinkle		
Onion powder, sprinkle		
Pepper, generous sprinkle		
Water	2 tbsp.	30 mL
Barbecue sauce (your choice)	2/3 cup	150 mL

Sprinkle ribs with garlic powder, onion powder and pepper. Place on wide, long sheet of heavy-duty foil.

Sprinkle ribs with water. Bring long sides of foil up over ribs and fold together several times. Crease to seal top. Press short sides of foil together at each end. Fold to seal packet well. Preheat gas barbecue to medium. Place packet on ungreased grill. Reduce heat to low. Cook for 1 1/2 hours, turning every 15 minutes, being careful not to pierce foil. Remove ribs from foil and place directly on barbecue grill over low heat.

Cook ribs for 15 to 20 minutes, brushing several times with barbecue sauce, until glazed and brown. Cut ribs apart to serve. Makes 6 to 7 ribs. Serves 6.

1 serving: 475 Calories; 39.1 g Total Fat (17.6 g Mono, 1.6 g Poly, 16.4 g Sat); 84 mg Cholesterol; 4 g Carbohydrate; 2 g Fibre; 25 g Protein; 282 mg Sodium

Savoury Chicken Pizza

A chicken dinner you can eat with your hands!

Ingredient	Imperial	Metric
Coarse dry bread crumbs	1/2 cup	125 mL
Onion flakes, crushed	2 1/4 tsp.	11 mL
Parsley flakes	1/4 tsp.	1 mL
Dried chives	1/4 tsp.	1 mL
Poultry seasoning	1/4 tsp.	1 mL
Chicken bouillon powder	1/4 tsp.	1 mL
Pepper, just a pinch		
Water	1/2 – 2/3 cup	125 – 150 mL
Partially baked pizza crust (or focaccia bread), 12 inch (30 cm) diameter	1	1
Chopped cooked chicken	2 cups	500 mL
Dried cranberries, soaked in boiling water for 15 minutes and drained	1/3 cup	75 mL
Grated part-skim mozzarella cheese	1 1/2 cups	375 mL
Prepared chicken gravy (your own or a mix), heated (optional)	1 1/2 cups	375 mL

Combine first 7 ingredients in small bowl. Stir in water, a bit at a time, until just spreading consistency.

Spread over crust.

Scatter chicken, cranberries and cheese over crumb mixture. Preheat gas barbecue to high. Turn off centre or left burner. Place pizza directly on greased grill over unlit burner. Close lid. Cook for 15 to 20 minutes, rotating pizza at halftime, until crust is golden and cheese is melted.

Serve with gravy for dipping. Cuts into 8 wedges.

1 wedge: 260 Calories; 8.2 g Total Fat (2.2 g Mono, 0.9 g Poly, 3.3 g Sat); 45 mg Cholesterol; 24 g Carbohydrate; 1 g Fibre; 21 g Protein; 404 mg Sodium

Sweet And Sour Chicken Pizza

The tart cranberry base enhances the sweet coating on the chicken.
Definitely a unique flavour sensation!

Boneless, skinless chicken breast halves (about 2), cut across grain into thin strips	1/2 lb.	225 g
Cooking oil	2 tsp.	10 mL
Prepared orange juice	2 tbsp.	30 mL
Soy sauce	2 tbsp.	30 mL
Brown sugar, packed	2 tbsp.	30 mL
Garlic powder, just a pinch		
Whole cranberry sauce, mashed	1/3 cup	75 mL
Prebaked pizza crust (or focaccia bread), 12 inch (30 cm) diameter	1	1
Grated part-skim mozzarella cheese	1 1/2 cups	375 mL
Green onions, sliced	2	2

Stir-fry chicken in cooking oil in small frying pan until no longer pink.

Add next 4 ingredients. Stir-fry until syrupy and chicken is coated.

Spread cranberry sauce over crust. Top with chicken mixture.

Scatter cheese and green onion over chicken. Preheat gas barbecue to high. Turn off centre or left burner. Place pizza directly on greased grill over unlit burner. Close lid. Cook for 15 to 20 minutes, rotating pizza at halftime, until crust is golden and cheese is melted. Cuts into 8 wedges.

1 wedge: 229 Calories; 6.6 g Total Fat (1.9 g Mono, 0.6 g Poly, 2.6 g Sat); 28 mg Cholesterol; 26 g Carbohydrate; trace Fibre; 16 g Protein; 556 mg Sodium

 tip *To help prevent sticking and create nice, even grill marks, don't move food around once placed on the greased grill until time to turn it. Starting with a clean grill also helps.*

Spiced Cornmeal Chicken

The yellow Cornmeal Coating is crunchy and attractive.
Serve with salsa or guacamole—or both!

CORNMEAL COATING

Yellow cornmeal	1/2 – 2/3 cup	125 – 150 mL
Ground cumin	1/2 – 1 tsp.	2 – 5 mL
Ground coriander	1/2 – 1 tsp.	2 – 5 mL
Pepper	1 tsp.	5 mL
Brown sugar, packed	1 tsp.	5 mL
Chili powder	1 tsp.	5 mL
Dried whole oregano	1 tsp.	5 mL
Salt	1/4 tsp.	1 mL
Boneless, skinless chicken breast halves (about 1 lb., 454 g)	4	4

Cornmeal Coating: Combine first 8 ingredients in shallow dish. Makes 2/3 cup (150 mL) coating.

Roll chicken in coating to cover completely. Preheat electric grill for 5 minutes or gas barbecue to medium. Place chicken on well-greased grill. Cook for about 5 minutes per side until no longer pink inside. Serves 4.

1 serving: 203 Calories; 2.5 g Total Fat (0.6 g Mono, 0.6 g Poly, 0.6 g Sat); 66 mg Cholesterol; 16 g Carbohydrate; 1 g Fibre; 27 g Protein; 157 mg Sodium

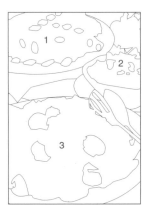

1. Dry Curry Ribs, page 114
2. Warm Potato Salad, page 120
3. Chicken And Artichoke Salad, page 93

Props Courtesy Of: Browne & Co. Ltd.

Main Dishes

Teriyaki Turkey Skewers

The tastes of turkey, pineapple and green pepper go well together.

SAUCE		
Teriyaki sauce	1/2 cup	125 mL
Liquid honey	2 tbsp.	30 mL
Ketchup	2 tbsp.	30 mL
Pepper	1 tsp.	5 mL
Ground ginger	1/4 – 1/2 tsp.	1 – 2 mL
Garlic powder	1/2 tsp.	2 mL
Cayenne pepper	1/8 – 1/4 tsp.	0.5 – 1 mL
Boneless, skinless turkey breast halves, cut into 3/4 – 1 inch (2 – 2.5 cm) pieces	1 1/2 lbs.	680 g
Fresh pineapple pieces, cut 3/4 inch (2 cm) thick	2 1/2 cups	625 mL
Green pepper, cut into 3/4 inch (2 cm) pieces	2 1/2 cups	625 mL
Bamboo skewers (12 inch, 30 cm, length), soaked in water for 10 minutes	10	10

Sauce: Combine first 7 ingredients in small bowl. Makes 1/2 cup (125 mL) basting sauce.

Preheat electric grill for 5 minutes or gas barbecue to medium. Thread turkey, pineapple and green pepper alternately onto skewers. Cook skewers on greased grill for 12 to 15 minutes, turning and brushing occasionally with sauce, until turkey is tender. Makes 10 skewers.

1 skewer: 136 Calories; 0.7 g Total Fat (0.1 g Mono, 0.2 g Poly, 0.2 g Sat); 42 mg Cholesterol; 15 g Carbohydrate; 1 g Fibre; 18 g Protein; 654 mg Sodium

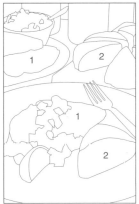

1. Lime Chicken And Salsa, page 56
2. Mexiscones, page 140

Props Courtesy Of: Pfaltzgraff Canada
Pier 1 Imports

Lime Chicken And Salsa

These chicken breasts are marinated in a sweet and spicy sauce.

LIME MARINADE

Sweet (or regular) chili sauce	2 tbsp.	30 mL
Peanut (or cooking) oil	1 tbsp.	15 mL
Lime juice	2 tbsp.	30 mL
Finely grated lime zest	1/2 tsp.	2 mL
Fish sauce	1 tsp.	5 mL
Brown sugar, packed	1 tsp.	5 mL
Finely grated gingerroot (or 1/4 tsp., 1 mL, ground ginger)	1 tsp.	5 mL
Garlic clove, minced (or 1/4 tsp., 1 mL, powder)	1	1
Salt	1/4 tsp.	1 mL
Boneless, skinless chicken breast halves (about 1 lb., 454 g)	4	4

GRILLED SALSA

Small red pepper, quartered	1	1
Can of pineapple slices, drained and 1 tbsp. (15 mL) juice reserved	14 oz.	398 mL
Small zucchini, with peel, cut lengthwise into 1/4 inch (6 mm) thick slices	1	1
Lime juice	1 tbsp.	15 mL
Reserved pineapple juice	1 tbsp.	15 mL
Peanut (or cooking) oil	1 tbsp.	15 mL
Chopped salted peanuts	3 tbsp.	50 mL
Garlic clove, minced (or 1/4 tsp., 1 mL, powder)	1	1
Salt	1/4 tsp.	1 mL

Lime Marinade: Combine first 9 ingredients in large bowl or resealable freezer bag. Makes about 1/2 cup (125 mL) marinade.

Add chicken. Turn to coat. Cover or seal. Marinate in refrigerator for 2 hours. Drain and discard marinade. Preheat electric grill for 5 minutes or gas barbecue to medium. Cook chicken on greased grill for about 5 minutes per side until no longer pink inside.

(continued on next page)

Grilled Salsa: Place red pepper, pineapple and zucchini on greased grill. Cook for 5 to 7 minutes, turning once, until grill marks appear and pepper and zucchini are tender-crisp. Finely chop pepper, pineapple and zucchini. Put into medium bowl.

Add remaining 6 ingredients. Stir. Makes about 2 1/2 cups (625 mL) salsa. Serve with chicken. Serves 4.

1 serving: 334 Calories; 10.2 g Total Fat (4.6 g Mono, 2.8 g Poly, 1.8 g Sat); 66 mg Cholesterol; 35 g Carbohydrate; 3 g Fibre; 28 g Protein; 372 mg Sodium

Pictured on page 54.

Balsamic Chili Chicken

*The flavours of rosemary and balsamic vinegar
are absorbed by this tender chicken.*

MARINADE

Balsamic vinegar	1/4 cup	60 mL
Olive (or cooking) oil	3 tbsp.	50 mL
Sweet (or regular) chili sauce	3 tbsp.	50 mL
Dried rosemary, crushed	1/2 tsp.	2 mL
Pepper	1/2 tsp.	2 mL
Garlic cloves, minced (or 1/2 tsp., 2 mL, powder)	2	2
Bone-in, skinless chicken thighs (about 2 1/2 lbs., 1.1 kg)	8	8

Marinade: Combine first 6 ingredients in jar with tight-fitting lid. Shake well. Pour into medium shallow dish or resealable freezer bag. Makes 3/4 cup (175 mL) marinade.

Add chicken. Turn to coat. Cover or seal. Marinate in refrigerator for at least 3 hours or overnight, turning occasionally. Drain, reserving marinade. Boil marinade in small saucepan for 5 minutes. Preheat gas barbecue to medium-low. Place chicken on greased grill. Close lid. Cook for about 10 minutes per side, brushing occasionally with marinade, until no longer pink inside. Serves 4.

1 serving: 294 Calories; 18.2 g Total Fat (10.6 g Mono, 2.7 g Poly, 3.6 g Sat); 101 mg Cholesterol; 5 g Carbohydrate; 1 g Fibre; 27 g Protein; 174 mg Sodium

Roasted Stuffed Turkey

A moist, succulent turkey stuffed with cashews, raisins and cranberry jelly.

CASHEW RAISIN STUFFING

Cooking oil	1 tbsp.	15 mL
Finely chopped onion	1 cup	250 mL
Coarse dry bread crumbs	4 cups	1 L
Cashews, toasted (see Tip, page 146), chopped	1 cup	250 mL
Raisins, coarsely chopped	1/2 cup	125 mL
Chopped fresh parsley (or 3 1/2 tsp., 17 mL, flakes)	1/3 cup	75 mL
Cranberry jelly, chopped	1/4 cup	60 mL
Hard margarine (or butter), melted	2 tbsp.	30 mL
Salt	1/4 tsp.	1 mL
Pepper	1/4 tsp.	1 mL
Whole turkey	8 – 10 lbs.	3.6 – 4.5 kg

ORANGE GLAZE

Prepared orange juice	2/3 cup	150 mL
Cranberry jelly	1/2 cup	125 mL
Brandy	2 tbsp.	30 mL
Hard margarine (or butter)	2 tbsp.	30 mL
Salt	1/4 tsp.	1 mL
Pepper	1/4 tsp.	1 mL

Cashew Raisin Stuffing: Heat cooking oil in small frying pan on medium-low. Cook onion for about 10 minutes, stirring occasionally, until soft. Put into large bowl.

Add next 8 ingredients. Mix well.

Loosely fill both body and neck cavities of turkey with stuffing. Secure with wooden picks or small metal skewers. Tie legs together. Fold wings behind. Preheat gas barbecue to medium. Place turkey on greased wire rack in roaster. Cover turkey (not roaster) loosely with greased foil. Place 1 cup (250 mL) water in bottom of roaster. Turn left or centre burner to low, leaving right burner on medium. Place roaster on ungreased grill over low burner. Close lid. Cook for 2 3/4 hours, adding more water as needed to roaster to prevent going dry.

(continued on next page)

Main Dishes

Orange Glaze: Combine all 6 ingredients in medium saucepan. Heat and stir on medium-high until jelly is melted. Makes 1 cup (250 mL) glaze. Remove foil from turkey. Brush turkey with glaze. Cook for 15 to 20 minutes, brushing frequently with glaze, until meat thermometer inserted in thigh reads 180°F (82°C). Let turkey stand for 15 minutes before carving. Remove stuffing from turkey. Makes about 4 cups (1 L) stuffing. Serve with turkey. Serves 10.

1 serving: 853 Calories; 29.8 g Total Fat (13.5 g Mono, 6.5 g Poly, 7.3 g Sat); 286 mg Cholesterol; 56 g Carbohydrate; 3 g Fibre; 85 g Protein; 758 mg Sodium

Barbecued Chicken Thighs

These tender, juicy morsels are nicely glazed with a slightly sweet and spicy marinade.

Boneless, skinless chicken thighs (about 1 1/2 lbs., 680 g)	12	12
Ketchup	1/4 cup	60 mL
White vinegar	1/4 cup	60 mL
Soy sauce	2 tbsp.	30 mL
Worcestershire sauce	1 tbsp.	15 mL
Dried crushed chilies	1 tsp.	5 mL
Granulated sugar	1 tbsp.	15 mL

Pound chicken flat to even thickness.

Combine remaining 6 ingredients in medium bowl or resealable freezer bag. Add chicken. Stir to coat. Cover or seal. Marinate in refrigerator for at least 2 hours or overnight. Drain and discard marinade. Preheat gas barbecue to medium. Place chicken on greased grill. Close lid. Cook for 20 to 25 minutes, turning once or twice, until tender and no longer pink inside. Serves 6.

1 serving: 175 Calories; 6.8 g Total Fat (2.1 g Mono, 1.7 g Poly, 1.7 g Sat); 103 mg Cholesterol; 3 g Carbohydrate; trace Fibre; 24 g Protein; 252 mg Sodium

Roasted Cornish Hens

These moist, nicely browned Cornish hens taste of apple and
sage with a hint of cinnamon. The perfect meal for entertaining.

Cornish hens (about 1 1/2 lbs., 680 g, each)	2	2
MARINADE		
Beer (or alcohol-free beer)	1 cup	250 mL
Applesauce	1/2 cup	125 mL
Olive (or cooking) oil	2 tbsp.	30 mL
Liquid honey	2 tbsp.	30 mL
Paprika	1 tsp.	5 mL
Ground sage	3/4 tsp.	4 mL
Ground cinnamon	1/2 tsp.	2 mL
Salt	1/4 tsp.	1 mL

Place 1 Cornish hen, breast-side down, on cutting board. Using kitchen shears or sharp knife, cut down both sides of backbone to remove. Turn hen, breast-side up. Cut lengthwise through breast into halves. Repeat with other hen.

Marinade: Combine all 8 ingredients in large bowl or resealable freezer bag. Add Cornish hens. Turn to coat. Cover or seal. Marinate in refrigerator for at least 6 hours or overnight. Drain, reserving marinade. Boil marinade in small saucepan for 5 minutes. Preheat gas barbecue to high. Turn off centre or left burner. Place Cornish hen halves, bone-side down, on greased grill over unlit burner. Brush with marinade. Close lid. Cook for 20 minutes. Turn. Cook for about 20 minutes, brushing with marinade occasionally, until skin is browned and meat is no longer pink inside. Serves 4.

1 serving: 687 Calories; 45.5 g Total Fat (22 g Mono, 8.3 g Poly, 11.6 g Sat); 277 mg Cholesterol; 15 g Carbohydrate; 1 g Fibre; 48 g Protein; 288 mg Sodium

Red Currant Chicken Skewers

Kids and adults alike will enjoy the nice, sweet flavour of these skewers.
Serve with a fresh green salad.

RED CURRANT MARINADE

Red currant jelly	1/3 cup	75 mL
Grainy mustard	3 tbsp.	50 mL
Lime juice	2 tbsp.	30 mL
Cooking oil	2 tbsp.	30 mL
Soy sauce	1 tsp.	5 mL
Garlic salt	1/2 tsp.	2 mL
Boneless, skinless chicken breast halves (about 4), cut across grain into 1/8 inch (3 mm) slices	1 lb.	454 g
Bamboo skewers (8 inch, 20 cm, length), soaked in water for 10 minutes	16	16

Red Currant Marinade: Combine first 6 ingredients in medium bowl or resealable freezer bag. Makes about 1/3 cup (75 mL) marinade.

Add chicken. Stir to coat. Cover or seal. Marinate in refrigerator for at least 8 hours or overnight. Drain and discard marinade.

Thread chicken, accordion-style, onto skewers. Preheat electric grill for 5 minutes or gas barbecue to medium. Cook skewers on greased grill for about 10 minutes, turning several times, until chicken is tender and no longer pink. Makes 16 skewers.

1 skewer: 49 Calories; 1.5 g Total Fat (0.6 g Mono, 0.4 g Poly, 0.2 g Sat); 16 mg Cholesterol; 2 g Carbohydrate; trace Fibre; 7 g Protein; 51 mg Sodium

Paré Pointer

Children are a comfort in your old age and they help you reach it sooner.

Butterflied Chicken

Excellent roasted flavour in this grilled stuffed chicken.

Hard margarine (or butter), softened	3 tbsp.	50 mL
Worcestershire sauce	1 tbsp.	15 mL
Liquid honey	1 tbsp.	15 mL
Lemon pepper	2 tsp.	10 mL
Dried whole oregano	3/4 tsp.	4 mL
Garlic cloves, minced (or 1/2 tsp., 2 mL, powder)	2	2
Whole roasting chicken	3 1/2 lbs.	1.6 kg

Combine first 6 ingredients in small bowl.

Place chicken, breast-side down, on cutting board. Using kitchen shears or sharp knife, cut down both sides of backbone to remove. Turn chicken, breast-side up. Press chicken out flat. Carefully loosen, but do not remove, skin from chicken. Stuff margarine mixture between flesh and skin, spreading mixture as evenly as possible. Preheat gas barbecue to medium. Turn off centre or left burner. Place chicken, stuffed side down, on greased grill over drip pan on unlit side. Close lid. Cook for 35 minutes. Carefully turn chicken. Cook for 55 to 60 minutes until meat thermometer inserted in thigh reads 180°F (82°C). Let stand for 15 minutes. Cut into serving-size pieces. Serves 4 to 6.

1 serving: 738 Calories; 45 g Total Fat (19.9 g Mono, 8.8 g Poly, 11.9 g Sat); 234 mg Cholesterol; 6 g Carbohydrate; trace Fibre; 73 g Protein; 367 mg Sodium

---

Paré Pointer

Usually a teacher's worst-behaved student has a perfect attendance record.

Main Dishes

Satay Rib Chops

These tender pork chops taste of peanuts and spices.
Serve with basmati rice or another type of aromatic rice.

SATAY MARINADE

Smooth peanut butter	1/2 cup	125 mL
Apple juice	2/3 cup	150 mL
Hot water	1/4 cup	60 mL
Lime juice	2 tbsp.	30 mL
Soy sauce	1 tbsp.	15 mL
Dried crushed chilies	1 tsp.	5 mL
Ground coriander	1/2 – 1 tsp.	2 – 5 mL
Pepper	1/4 tsp.	1 mL
Garlic cloves, minced (or 1/2 tsp., 2 mL, powder)	2	2
Pork rib chops (about 8 oz., 225 g, each)	4	4

Satay Marinade: Combine first 9 ingredients in medium shallow dish or resealable freezer bag. Makes 1 1/3 cups (325 mL) marinade.

Add chops. Turn to coat. Cover or seal. Marinate in refrigerator for at least 6 hours or overnight. Drain, reserving marinade. Boil marinade in small saucepan for 5 minutes. Preheat electric grill for 5 minutes or gas barbecue to medium. Cook chops on well-greased grill for 7 to 8 minutes per side, basting with reserved marinade, until tender. Serves 4.

1 serving: 520 Calories; 34.8 g Total Fat (16 g Mono, 6.1 g Poly, 9.9 g Sat); 91 mg Cholesterol; 13 g Carbohydrate; 2 g Fibre; 41 g Protein; 497 mg Sodium

Pictured on page 72.

Paré Pointer

Increase the size of your pay cheque with a magnifying glass.

Stuffed Pork Chops

The bacon and blue cheese stuffing goes very well with the juicy pork.

BLUE CHEESE STUFFING

Chopped onion	1 cup	250 mL
Bacon slices, diced	4	4
Chopped fresh mushrooms	1 cup	250 mL
Crumbled blue cheese	1/3 cup	75 mL
Parsley flakes	1/2 tsp.	2 mL
Chopped fresh chives (or 1/4 tsp., 1 mL, dried)	1 tsp.	5 mL
Fine dry bread crumbs	1/4 cup	60 mL
Thick pork loin chops, bone in (about 6 – 7 oz., 170 – 200 g, each), trimmed of fat	6	6
Cooking oil	1 tbsp.	15 mL

Blue Cheese Stuffing: Sauté onion and bacon in frying pan until onion is soft.

Add mushrooms. Sauté until golden. Remove from heat. Cool slightly.

Add next 4 ingredients. Mix well. Makes about 2 cups (500 mL) stuffing.

Cut horizontal slit in meaty part of each chop towards bone. Pack 1/3 cup (75 mL) stuffing into each opening. Secure with wooden picks. Brush chops with cooking oil. Preheat electric grill for 5 minutes or gas barbecue to medium. Cook chops on greased grill for 10 to 15 minutes per side until desired doneness. Remove wooden picks. Makes 6 stuffed pork chops.

1 stuffed pork chop: 317 Calories; 18.4 g Total Fat (9.9 g Mono, 2.6 g Poly, 8.1 g Sat); 84 mg Cholesterol; 7 g Carbohydrate; 1 g Fibre; 30 g Protein; 297 mg Sodium

 To make "diamond" grill marks, place food on preheated grill without moving around. Halfway through cooking, lift and turn food 1/8 turn (45 degrees). Set back on grill without moving around. See photos on pages 36, 54, 72, 126 and 144. To make "square" grill marks, turn food 1/4 turn (90 degrees).

Main Dishes

Balsamic Chops

The addition of balsamic vinegar adds a subtle tang.
The Pecan And Blue Cheese Butter lends a richness to every bite.

PECAN AND BLUE CHEESE BUTTER

Butter (or hard margarine), softened	1/3 cup	75 mL
Blue cheese, crumbled	2 oz.	57 g
Pecans, toasted (see Tip, page 146) and finely chopped	1/4 cup	60 mL
Ground cinnamon	1/8 tsp.	0.5 mL
Chopped fresh chives (or 1 1/2 tsp., 7 mL, dried)	2 tbsp.	30 mL
Balsamic vinegar	1/3 cup	75 mL
Olive (or cooking) oil	2 tbsp.	30 mL
Orange marmalade, warmed	1 tbsp.	15 mL
Pork loin chops, bone in (about 6 – 7 oz., 170 – 200 g, each)	4	4

Pecan And Blue Cheese Butter: Combine first 5 ingredients in small bowl. Place on 12 inch (30 cm) square of waxed paper. Using waxed paper as guide, shape into 4 inch (10 cm) log. Chill for at least 1 hour until firm. Cut into eight 1/2 inch (12 mm) rounds.

Combine next 3 ingredients in medium shallow dish or resealable freezer bag. Makes 1/2 cup (125 mL) marinade.

Add chops. Turn to coat. Cover or seal. Marinate in refrigerator for 3 hours. Drain and discard marinade. Preheat electric grill for 5 minutes or gas barbecue to medium. Cook chops on greased grill for 5 to 8 minutes per side until desired doneness. Place 2 rounds of butter mixture on top of each hot chop. Serves 4.

1 serving: 739 Calories; 53.7 g Total Fat (22.7 g Mono, 4.2 g Poly, 22.7 g Sat); 210 mg Cholesterol; 4 g Carbohydrate; 1 g Fibre; 58 g Protein; 475 mg Sodium

Spicy Rubbed Tenderloin

Moist pork tenderloin with a dark red, spicy coating.

SPICE RUB		
Brown sugar, packed	2 tbsp.	30 mL
Paprika	2 tbsp.	30 mL
Dry mustard	2 tsp.	10 mL
Seasoned salt	1 tsp.	5 mL
Lemon pepper	1/2 tsp.	2 mL
Cayenne pepper	1/4 tsp.	1 mL
Pork tenderloin	1 lb.	454 g

Spice Rub: Combine first 6 ingredients in small bowl. Makes about 1/4 cup (60 mL) rub.

Cut pork lengthwise in half, almost, but not quite, through to other side. Open pork along cut and press to flatten evenly. Coat heavily on all sides with spice mixture. Rub or press spices in with heel of hand. Preheat electric grill for 5 minutes or gas barbecue to medium. Cook pork for about 10 minutes per side until desired doneness. Let stand on cutting board, tented with foil, for 10 minutes. Slice thinly to serve. Serves 4.

1 serving: 183 Calories; 5.7 g Total Fat (2.5 g Mono, 0.8 g Poly, 1.7 g Sat); 66 mg Cholesterol; 10 g Carbohydrate; 1 g Fibre; 23 g Protein; 341 mg Sodium

tip To crush peppercorns, place whole peppercorns in a small plastic bag. Tap peppercorns with a heavy object, such as a meat mallet or hammer, until coarsely crushed.

Pork And Pepper Skewers

Serve these sweet and colourful skewers with rice.

SWEET AND SOUR MARINADE

Pineapple juice	1/2 cup	125 mL
Ketchup	1/3 cup	75 mL
White vinegar	2 tbsp.	30 mL
Soy sauce	2 tbsp.	30 mL
Brown sugar, packed	1 tbsp.	15 mL
Lemon pepper	1 tbsp.	15 mL
Garlic powder	1 tsp.	5 mL
Pork tenderloin, cut into 3/4 inch (2 cm) cubes	1 1/2 lbs.	680 g
Large red peppers, cut into 3/4 inch (2 cm) pieces	1 – 2	1 – 2
Large yellow peppers, cut into 3/4 inch (2 cm) pieces	1 – 2	1 – 2
Bamboo skewers (12 inch, 30 cm, length), soaked in water for 10 minutes	8	8

Sweet And Sour Marinade: Combine first 7 ingredients in shallow dish or resealable freezer bag. Makes 1 1/3 cups (325 mL) marinade.

Add pork. Turn to coat. Cover or seal. Marinate in refrigerator for at least 3 hours or overnight. Drain, reserving marinade. Boil marinade in small saucepan for 5 minutes.

Thread pork and red and yellow pepper alternately onto skewers. Preheat gas barbecue to medium. Cook skewers on greased grill for about 20 minutes, turning occasionally and basting with reserved marinade, until pork is tender. Makes 8 skewers.

1 skewer: 162 Calories; 4.2 g Total Fat (1.7 g Mono, 0.4 g Poly, 1.5 g Sat); 54 mg Cholesterol; 11 g Carbohydrate; 1 g Fibre; 19 g Protein; 425 mg Sodium

Five-Spice Ribs

Spicy, glazed ribs with a scrumptious flavour.
Messy to eat—and that's half of the fun!

Pork side ribs, cut into 4 portions	4 lbs.	1.8 kg
Large onion, quartered	1	1
Bay leaves	2	2
Garlic cloves	6	6
Sherry (or alcohol-free sherry)	1 cup	250 mL
Water, to cover		
SAUCE		
Indonesian sweet (or thick) soy sauce	1/4 cup	60 mL
Fancy (mild) molasses	3 tbsp.	50 mL
Lemon juice	2 tbsp.	30 mL
Celery seed	1 tsp.	5 mL
Paprika	1 tsp.	5 mL
Hot pepper sauce	1 tsp.	5 mL
Chinese five-spice powder	2 tsp.	10 mL

Put first 5 ingredients into stock pot or Dutch oven. Add enough water just to cover ribs. Bring to a boil. Cover. Reduce heat to medium-low. Simmer for 45 to 60 minutes until ribs are tender. Drain.

Sauce: Combine all 7 ingredients in small bowl. Makes 2/3 cup (150 mL) basting sauce. Brush ribs with sauce. Preheat gas barbecue to medium-low. Place ribs on well-greased grill. Cook for about 5 minutes per side, basting with remaining sauce often, until glazed and browned. Serves 4.

1 serving: 878 Calories; 61.1 g Total Fat (26.4 g Mono, 5.6 g Poly, 23.1 g Sat); 234 mg Cholesterol; 13 g Carbohydrate; trace Fibre; 65 g Protein; 1156 mg Sodium

tip   *To prevent flare-ups and burning and to allow the meat to brown evenly to obtain the more professional and visually-appealing grill lines, trim excess fat from meat before cooking.*

Glazed Ham And Pineapple

The slight sweetness of the marinade helps to balance the saltiness of the ham.
The dark grill marks are very attractive.

MARINADE		
Pineapple juice	3/4 cup	175 mL
Soy sauce	1 tbsp.	15 mL
Liquid honey	1 tbsp.	15 mL
Prepared mustard	1 tsp.	5 mL
Ground cloves	1/8 tsp.	0.5 mL
Garlic powder	1/4 tsp.	1 mL
Small ham steaks (about 4 oz., 113 g, each), see Note	6	6
Canned (or fresh) pineapple slices	6	6

Marinade: Mix first 6 ingredients in shallow dish or resealable freezer bag. Makes about 1 cup (250 mL) marinade.

Add ham. Turn to coat. Cover or seal. Marinate in refrigerator for 2 hours. Drain, reserving marinade. Boil marinade in small saucepan for 5 minutes.

Preheat gas barbecue to medium-high. Place ham and pineapple on greased grill. Cook for 5 to 10 minutes, turning and brushing with reserved marinade, until ham is golden and heated through. Serves 6.

1 serving: 189 Calories; 5 g Total Fat (22 g Mono, 0.6 g Poly, 1.6 g Sat); 51 mg Cholesterol; 13 g Carbohydrate; 1 g Fibre; 23 g Protein; 1622 mg Sodium

Note: If only large ham steaks are available, cut them into serving-size pieces after grilling.

Sweet Pork Tenderloin

Mildly flavoured pork with a delicious, tangy coating around the edges.

MARINADE		
Ketchup	1/2 cup	125 mL
Worcestershire sauce	1/4 cup	60 mL
Brown sugar, packed	1/4 cup	60 mL
Malt vinegar	1/4 cup	60 mL
Prepared orange juice	1/4 cup	60 mL
Grainy mustard	2 tbsp.	30 mL
Garlic cloves, minced (or 1/2 tsp., 2 mL, powder)	2	2
Dried rosemary, crushed	1/2 tsp.	2 mL
Pork tenderloin	2 lbs.	900 g

Marinade: Combine first 8 ingredients in medium shallow dish or resealable freezer bag. Makes about 1 1/2 cups (375 mL) marinade.

Add pork. Turn to coat. Cover or seal. Marinate in refrigerator for at least 6 hours or overnight. Drain and discard marinade. Preheat gas barbecue to medium-low. Place pork on greased grill. Close lid. Cook for about 40 minutes, turning every 5 minutes, until no longer pink inside. Serves 8.

1 serving: 213 Calories; 5.7 g Total Fat (2.3 g Mono, 0.7 g Poly, 2 g Sat); 71 mg Cholesterol; 14 g Carbohydrate; trace Fibre; 25 g Protein; 388 mg Sodium

1. Barbecued Asparagus, page 124
2. Sweet Orange Salmon, page 104

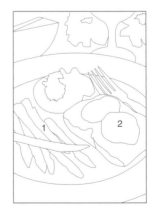

Fiery Chipotle Lamb

Glazed and lightly browned lamb with a warm heat
from the chipotle (chih-POHT-lay) chili peppers.

CHIPOTLE SPREAD

Cooking oil	1 tbsp.	15 mL
Chopped onion	1 cup	250 mL
Garlic cloves, minced (or 1/2 tsp., 2 mL, powder)	2	2
Mayonnaise (not salad dressing)	1/3 cup	75 mL
Chipotle chili peppers (see Note)	2 – 3	2 – 3
Granulated sugar	1 tbsp.	15 mL
Salt	1/2 tsp.	2 mL
Leg of lamb, bone in	3 1/3 lbs.	1.5 kg

Chipotle Spread: Heat cooking oil in medium frying pan on medium-low. Add onion and garlic. Heat and stir for about 10 minutes until onion is soft. Transfer to blender.

Add next 4 ingredients. Process until smooth. Makes 3/4 cup (175 mL) spread.

Place lamb in large shallow dish. Spread onion mixture over lamb. Cover. Marinate in refrigerator for up to 24 hours. Preheat gas barbecue to high. Turn off centre or left burner. Place lamb on greased grill over drip pan on unlit side. Close lid. Cook for about 2 hours until internal temperature reads at least 150°F (65°C) or until desired doneness. Serves 6 to 8.

1 serving: 642 Calories; 45.1 g Total Fat (20.8 g Mono, 6.5 g Poly, 14.7 g Sat); 190 mg Cholesterol; 5 g Carbohydrate; 1 g Fibre; 51 g Protein; 395 mg Sodium

Note: Available in Mexican section of grocery stores.

1. Satay Rib Chops, page 63
2. Veggie Bread Kabobs, page 123

Props Courtesy Of: The Bay

Main Dishes

Kefta Wraps

In Middle Eastern countries, well-seasoned, grilled ground lamb is a traditional meal when served in warm pita breads with a mint and yogurt sauce.

KEFTA

Lean ground lamb	1 lb.	454 g
Finely chopped green onion	1/4 cup	60 mL
Garlic cloves, minced (or 1/2 tsp., 2 mL, powder)	2	2
Sweet chili sauce	1 tbsp.	15 mL
Finely chopped fresh parsley (or 1 1/2 tsp., 7 mL, flakes)	2 tbsp.	30 mL
Finely chopped fresh mint leaves (or 3/4 tsp., 4 mL, dried)	1 tbsp.	15 mL
Seasoned salt	1 tsp.	5 mL
Ground cumin	1 tsp.	5 mL
Pepper	1/4 tsp.	1 mL
Bamboo skewers (8 inch, 20 cm, length), soaked in water for 10 minutes	6	6

YOGURT MINT SAUCE

Plain yogurt (not non-fat)	3/4 cup	175 mL
Green onion, finely chopped	1	1
Chopped fresh mint leaves (or 1 1/2 tsp., 7 mL, dried)	2 tbsp.	30 mL
Lemon juice	1 tbsp.	15 mL
Sweet chili sauce	2 tsp.	10 mL
Salt	1/4 tsp.	1 mL
Indian Naan Bread, page 24 (or warm pita breads)	6	6
Shredded lettuce (your choice)	3/4 cup	175 mL
Small yellow or orange pepper, slivered	1	1
Small tomato, seeds removed, diced	1	1

Kefta: Combine first 9 ingredients in large bowl until well mixed. Divide into 6 portions. Using wet hands, form into 6 inch (15 cm) cigar-like shapes.

(continued on next page)

Main Dishes

Push lengthwise onto skewers until skewer just shows through. Preheat electric grill for 5 minutes or gas barbecue to medium. Cook skewers on greased grill for about 10 minutes, rotating a quarter turn several times, until lamb is well browned and no longer pink inside.

Yogurt Mint Sauce: Stir first 6 ingredients in small bowl. Chill for 30 minutes to blend flavours. Makes scant 1 cup (250 mL) sauce.

Spoon about 2 tbsp. (30 mL) sauce across centre of each bread. Divide and layer kefta, lettuce, yellow pepper and tomato over sauce. Fold bread sides to centre to enclose. Wrap tightly in waxed paper to serve. Serves 6.

1 serving: 319 Calories; 5.9 g Total Fat (2 g Mono, 0.8 g Poly, 2 g Sat); 56 mg Cholesterol; 41 g Carbohydrate; 2 g Fibre; 25 g Protein; 766 mg Sodium

Pictured on page 89.

Lemon Herb Lamb Chops

Perfectly seasoned, moist chops flavoured with lemon and herbs.

LEMON HERB MARINADE

Lemon juice	3 tbsp.	50 mL
Finely grated lemon zest	1 tsp.	5 mL
Parsley flakes	1 tbsp.	15 mL
Liquid honey	1 tbsp.	15 mL
Dried oregano	1/2 tsp.	2 mL
Dried crushed chilies	3/4 tsp.	4 mL
Olive (or cooking) oil	3 tbsp.	50 mL
Salt	1/2 tsp.	2 mL
Pepper	1/4 tsp.	1 mL
Garlic cloves, minced (or 1/2 tsp., 2 mL, powder)	2	2
Lamb chops (about 1 lb., 454 g)	8	8

Lemon Herb Marinade: Combine first 10 ingredients in medium shallow dish or resealable freezer bag. Makes about 1/2 cup (125 mL) marinade.

Add lamb chops. Turn to coat. Cover or seal. Marinate in refrigerator for at least 6 hours or overnight, turning occasionally. Drain and discard marinade. Preheat electric grill for 5 minutes or gas barbecue to medium. Cook lamb chops on greased grill for 5 to 7 minutes per side until desired doneness. Serves 4.

1 serving: 286 Calories; 22.6 g Total Fat (10.9 g Mono, 1.8 g Poly, 8.2 g Sat); 70 mg Cholesterol; 3 g Carbohydrate; trace Fibre; 17 g Protein; 199 mg Sodium

Cornmeal-Crusted Salmon

A seasoned, crunchy, golden coating keeps the salmon moist as it grills to perfection.

CORNMEAL COATING

Yellow cornmeal	1/3 cup	75 mL
Onion powder	1 tsp.	5 mL
Paprika	1 tsp.	5 mL
Seasoned salt	3/4 tsp.	4 mL
Dried thyme, crushed	1/2 tsp.	2 mL
Garlic powder (optional)	1/4 tsp.	1 mL
Hard margarine (or butter)	3 tbsp.	50 mL
Lemon juice	2 tsp.	10 mL
Centre-cut salmon fillets (about 1 1/4 lbs., 560 g), skin removed	4	4

Cornmeal Coating: Combine first 6 ingredients in shallow dish.

Melt margarine in small saucepan. Stir in lemon juice.

Pat salmon dry with paper towels. Dip into margarine mixture to coat all sides. Roll in cornmeal mixture. Preheat electric grill for 5 minutes or gas barbecue to medium. Cook salmon on greased grill for 10 to 15 minutes, turning carefully after 6 minutes, until salmon flakes easily when tested with fork. Serves 4.

1 serving: 383 Calories; 24.2 g Total Fat (11.1 g Mono, 6.5 g Poly, 4.9 g Sat); 83 mg Cholesterol; 11 g Carbohydrate; 1 g Fibre; 29 g Protein; 408 mg Sodium

 tip

To make your own drip pan, use a large piece of heavy-duty foil. Fold all four edges over twice, about 1 1/2 inches (3.8 cm) each time. Take folded portions and bend up at right angles to bottom, forming sides. Mitre (bend) corners to reinforce.

Main Dishes

Fish And Fennel Parcels

Aromatic, subtly flavoured fennel with the
bright addition of sun-dried tomatoes.

Cooking oil	1 tbsp.	15 mL
Fennel bulb (white part only), thinly sliced	1	1
Garlic clove, minced (or 1/4 tsp., 1 mL, powder)	1	1
Dry white (or alcohol-free) wine	1/2 cup	125 mL
Finely grated orange zest	1/2 tsp.	2 mL
Hard margarine (or butter), melted	4 tsp.	20 mL
Salt	1/4 tsp.	1 mL
Pepper	1/4 tsp.	1 mL
Snapper fillets (about 1 lb., 454 g)	4	4
Sun-dried tomatoes in oil, drained and finely chopped	1/3 cup	75 mL

Heat cooking oil in large frying pan on medium-low. Add fennel and garlic. Cook for about 10 minutes, stirring often, until fennel is soft and lightly browned.

Combine next 5 ingredients in small bowl.

Lay out 4 sheets of heavy-duty (or double layer of regular) foil about 16 inches (40 cm) long (depending on length of fillets). Divide fennel mixture among foil. Layer fish on top. Drizzle with wine mixture.

Scatter sun-dried tomatoes over fish. Bring up short sides of foil to meet over fish. Fold foil downwards several times to seal very well. Fold sides in and secure firmly. Preheat gas barbecue to medium. Place packets on ungreased grill. Close lid. Cook for about 10 minutes until fish flakes easily when tested with fork. Serves 4.

1 serving: 232 Calories; 9.1 g Total Fat (4.9 g Mono, 2 g Poly, 1.4 g Sat); 42 mg Cholesterol; 8 g Carbohydrate; trace Fibre; 25 g Protein; 398 mg Sodium

Bacon And Pineapple Scallops

The bacon lends a pleasant smoky flavour to the scallops and pineapple.
The moist scallops are glazed beautifully in a Polynesian-style marinade.

Indonesian sweet (or thick) soy sauce	1/2 cup	125 mL
Sweet (or regular) chili sauce	1/4 cup	60 mL
Cooking oil	2 tbsp.	30 mL
Lemon juice	1 tbsp.	15 mL
Fresh (or frozen, thawed) sea scallops (about 3/4 lb., 340 g)	16	16
Bacon slices, cut into 3 pieces each	8	8
Fresh pineapple, peeled and cut into 3/4 inch (2 cm) cubes (32 pieces)	1	1
Bamboo skewers (8 inch, 20 cm, length), soaked in water for 10 minutes	8	8

Combine soy sauce, chili sauce, cooking oil and lemon juice in shallow dish or resealable freezer bag. Remove and set aside 1/3 cup (75 mL) marinade for basting. Add scallops to remaining marinade. Stir to coat. Cover or seal. Marinate in refrigerator for 30 minutes. Drain and discard marinade.

Partially cook bacon in large frying pan on medium for about 4 minutes, turning once, until just starting to brown. Drain.

Thread 4 pieces of pineapple, 3 pieces of folded bacon and 2 scallops alternately onto each skewer, beginning and ending with pineapple. Preheat electric grill for 5 minutes or gas barbecue to medium. Cook skewers on greased grill for about 10 minutes, turning and brushing with reserved marinade, until scallops are firm and cooked through. Makes 8 skewers. Serves 4.

1 serving: 235 Calories; 10.7 g Total Fat (5.1 g Mono, 2.1 g Poly, 2.6 g Sat); 36 mg Cholesterol; 16 g Carbohydrate; 2 g Fibre; 19 g Protein; 1306 mg Sodium

Stuffed Salmon

The bacon gives the salmon a delicious smoky aftertaste
that is complemented by the mild-flavoured stuffing.

Whole salmon (or other fish), pan ready	3 lbs.	1.4 kg
Salt, sprinkle		

STUFFING		
Hard margarine (or butter)	2 tbsp.	30 mL
Chopped onion	1/2 cup	125 mL
Finely chopped celery	1/4 cup	60 mL
Fine dry bread crumbs	3/4 cup	175 mL
Parsley flakes	1/2 tsp.	2 mL
Poultry seasoning	1/2 tsp.	2 mL
Salt	1/4 tsp.	1 mL
Pepper, just a pinch		
Water		
Bacon slices	4	4

Rinse fish cavity. Pat dry with paper towels. Sprinkle inside with salt.

Stuffing: Melt margarine in frying pan on medium-high. Sauté onion and celery until soft. Remove from heat.

Add next 5 ingredients. Mix well. Add water only if necessary, a little bit at a time, just until stuffing holds together slightly when squeezed. Stuff fish. Secure opening with small skewers and string or wooden picks placed approximately every 1 1/2 inches (3.8 cm). Trim wooden picks, if necessary, to prevent puncturing foil. Set fish on large sheet of heavy-duty (or double layer of regular) foil.

Lay bacon on top. Wrap securely. Preheat gas barbecue to high. Place packet on ungreased grill. Close lid. Cook for about 10 minutes per side until fish flakes easily when tested with fork. Serves 6.

1 serving: 278 Calories; 16.5 g Total Fat (9.3 g Mono, 3.9 g Poly, 5.7 g Sat); 54 mg Cholesterol; 12 g Carbohydrate; 1 g Fibre; 19 g Protein; 402 mg Sodium

Grilled Crab Legs

Richly flavoured crab legs are delicately seasoned with herbs.

Fresh (or frozen, thawed) cooked Alaskan crab legs (about 9 oz., 255 g)	12	12
Hard margarine (or butter)	1/3 cup	75 mL
Chopped fresh parsley (or 1 1/2 tsp., 7 mL, flakes)	2 tbsp.	30 mL
Finely chopped green onion	2 tbsp.	30 mL
Lemon pepper	1 tsp.	5 mL

Split each crab leg on underside.

Melt margarine in small saucepan. Add remaining 3 ingredients. Brush cut side of crab with 2 tbsp. (30 mL) margarine mixture. Preheat gas barbecue to medium-high. Place crab on greased grill. Close lid. Cook for about 8 minutes, turning occasionally, until crab is hot. Serve remaining margarine mixture with crab for dipping. Makes 12 crab legs.

1 crab leg: 191 Calories; 7.6 g Total Fat (3.8 g Mono, 1.3 g Poly, 1.3 g Sat); 78 mg Cholesterol; trace Carbohydrate; trace Fibre; 29 g Protein; 1639 mg Sodium

Apricot-Stuffed Trout

The slight sweetness of the dill and apricot filling goes very well with the trout.

Cooking oil	2 tsp.	10 mL
Finely chopped red onion	1/4 cup	60 mL
Cooked jasmine rice	1/2 cup	125 mL
Pecans, toasted (see Tip, page 146) and finely chopped	2 tbsp.	30 mL
Prepared orange juice	1 tbsp.	15 mL
Finely chopped dried apricots	1 tbsp.	15 mL
Chopped fresh dill (or 1/2 tsp., 2 mL, dill weed)	1 1/2 tsp.	7 mL
Salt	1/4 tsp.	1 mL
Pepper, just a pinch		

(continued on next page)

| Whole trout, pan ready (about 1 1/4 lbs., 560 g) | 2 | 2 |

Heat cooking oil in small frying pan on medium-low. Cook red onion for about 10 minutes, stirring occasionally, until soft.

Combine next 7 ingredients in large bowl. Add onion. Mix well.

Rinse cavity of each fish. Pat dry with paper towels. Divide and fill cavities with rice mixture. Secure opening with small metal skewers or butcher's string. Preheat gas barbecue to medium-low. Place trout on well-greased grill. Close lid. Cook for 5 to 6 minutes per side until fish flakes easily when tested with fork. Serves 2.

1 serving: 311 Calories; 14.9 g Total Fat (7.4 g Mono, 4.4 g Poly, 2.2 g Sat); 55 mg Cholesterol; 22 g Carbohydrate; 1 g Fibre; 22 g Protein; 331 mg Sodium

Sweet Scallop Skewers

Tender, grilled scallops flavoured with orange zest and honey.

Fresh (or frozen, thawed) scallops, cut into 1/2 inch (12 mm) thick pieces	1 lb.	454 g
Bamboo skewers (8 inch, 20 cm, length), soaked in water for 10 minutes	8	8
Liquid honey	2 tbsp.	30 mL
Dijon mustard	2 tbsp.	30 mL
Salt	1/4 tsp.	1 mL
Finely grated orange zest	1/4 tsp.	1 mL
Chili powder	1/4 tsp.	1 mL

Thread scallops onto skewers.

Combine remaining 5 ingredients in small bowl. Brush scallops with honey mixture. Preheat electric grill for 5 minutes or gas barbecue to medium. Cook skewers on greased grill for about 8 minutes, turning and brushing several times with honey mixture, until scallops are opaque. Do not overcook. Makes 8 skewers.

1 skewer: 70 Calories; 0.7 g Total Fat (0.1 g Mono, 0.3 g Poly, 0.1 g Sat); 19 mg Cholesterol; 6 g Carbohydrate; trace Fibre; 10 g Protein; 219 mg Sodium

Cedar Plank Salmon

You will love the light smoky flavour of this salmon.
Perfectly complemented by a mild maple syrup sweetness.

Cedar plank (see Note)	1	1
Rye	1 cup	250 mL
Maple (or maple-flavoured) syrup	1/2 cup	125 mL
Low-sodium soy sauce	1/3 cup	75 mL
Olive (or cooking) oil	1/4 cup	60 mL
Parsley flakes	1/4 cup	60 mL
Chili sauce	3 tbsp.	50 mL
Pepper	1 tsp.	5 mL
Side of salmon, skin removed (or 8 salmon fillets, 4 oz., 113 g, each)	2 lbs.	900 g

Soak cedar plank in water for at least 8 hours or overnight, turning several times to soak both sides or weigh down with heavy object to keep submerged.

Combine next 7 ingredients in shallow dish.

Add fish. Turn to coat. Cover. Marinate in refrigerator for up to 24 hours. Drain and discard marinade. Preheat gas barbecue to medium-low. Place salmon on cedar plank on ungreased grill. Close lid. Cook for 15 to 30 minutes (depending on thickness of fish) until fish flakes easily when tested with fork. Serves 8.

1 serving: 259 Calories; 10.6 g Total Fat (4.9 g Mono, 3.2 g Poly, 1.6 g Sat); 62 mg Cholesterol; 8 g Carbohydrate; trace Fibre; 23 g Protein; 248 mg Sodium

Note: Purchase a cedar plank designed specifically for cooking food or an untreated cedar plank at least 1/2 inch (12 mm) thick.

Paré Pointer
Nobody notices your housework unless you don't do it.

Salmon And Pineapple

Pineapple and salmon make a lovely combination.
Garnish with green onion for a finished look.

PINEAPPLE AND TEQUILA SAUCE

Pineapple juice	1 1/2 cups	375 mL
Tequila	1/4 cup	60 mL
Prepared chicken broth	3 tbsp.	50 mL
Soy sauce	1 1/2 tbsp.	25 mL
Brown sugar, packed	1 tbsp.	15 mL
Pepper, just a pinch		
Water	1 tbsp.	15 mL
Cornstarch	1 tsp.	5 mL
Fresh pineapple, peeled and cut into 1 inch (2.5 cm) cubes (about 4 cups, 1 L)	1	1
Bamboo skewers (8 inch, 20 cm, length), soaked in water for 10 minutes	6	6
Brown sugar, packed	3 tbsp.	50 mL
Soy sauce	2 tbsp.	30 mL
Salmon steaks (about 8 oz., 225 g, each), cut 1 inch (2.5 cm) thick	6	6

Pineapple And Tequila Sauce: Combine first 6 ingredients in medium saucepan. Bring to a boil on medium-high. Boil, uncovered, for about 15 minutes until slightly thickened.

Stir water into cornstarch in small cup until smooth. Add to pineapple juice mixture. Heat and stir for 1 to 2 minutes until boiling and thickened. Makes about 1 1/4 cups (300 mL) sauce. Keep warm.

Thread 4 to 5 pineapple cubes onto each skewer. Preheat gas barbecue to medium-high. Place skewers on greased grill. Close lid. Cook for about 10 minutes, turning occasionally, until browned.

Combine second amounts of brown sugar and soy sauce in small bowl. Brush both sides of salmon with brown sugar mixture. Cook on greased grill for about 8 minutes per side until fish flakes easily when tested with fork. Serve pineapple with salmon. Drizzle with sauce. Serves 6.

1 serving: 474 Calories; 14.8 g Total Fat (4.8 g Mono, 5.9 g Poly, 2.3 g Sat); 124 mg Cholesterol; 33 g Carbohydrate; 1 g Fibre; 46 g Protein; 390 mg Sodium

Main Dishes

Seafood Pasta

Delicate seafood flavours accentuated by the tastes of wine and lemon. An attractive, inviting dish that is simply delicious.

Lemon juice	3 tbsp.	50 mL
Olive (or cooking) oil	1 tbsp.	15 mL
Pepper	1/4 tsp.	1 mL
Snapper fillets	3/4 lb.	340 g
Raw medium prawns, peeled and deveined	3/4 lb.	340 g
Fresh (or frozen, thawed) scallops	1/2 lb.	225 g
Large shell pasta	2 1/2 cups	625 mL
Boiling water	10 cups	2.5 L
Salt	1 tsp.	5 mL
Olive (or cooking) oil	1 tbsp.	15 mL
Finely chopped onion	3/4 cup	175 mL
Garlic clove, minced (or 1/4 tsp., 1 mL, powder)	1	1
Dry white (or alcohol-free) wine	1/2 cup	125 mL
Whipping cream	1 cup	250 mL
Salt	1/4 tsp.	1 mL
Frozen peas	1/2 cup	125 mL
Chopped fresh parsley (or 2 1/4 tsp., 11 mL, flakes)	3 tbsp.	50 mL
Finely grated fresh Parmesan cheese	1/4 cup	60 mL

Combine first 3 ingredients in medium bowl.

Add next 3 ingredients. Toss to coat. Preheat gas barbecue to medium. Place seafood on greased grill. Close lid. Cook for about 5 minutes, turning occasionally, until seafood is just cooked. Do not overcook. Chop snapper coarsely.

Cook pasta in boiling water and salt in large uncovered pot or Dutch oven for about 10 minutes, stirring occasionally, until pasta is tender but firm. Drain. Return to pot.

Heat second amount of olive oil in medium frying pan on medium-low. Add onion and garlic. Cook for about 10 minutes, stirring occasionally, until onion is soft.

(continued on next page)

Main Dishes

Add wine. Heat and stir for 2 to 3 minutes until almost all wine is evaporated.

Add whipping cream, salt and peas. Heat and stir for 3 to 5 minutes until thickened slightly and peas are hot. Add cream mixture and seafood to pasta.

Add parsley and Parmesan cheese. Stir. Makes about 8 cups (2 L).

1 cup (250 mL): 361 Calories; 16.2 g Total Fat (6 g Mono, 1.3 g Poly, 7.6 g Sat); 112 mg Cholesterol; 26 g Carbohydrate; 2 g Fibre; 26 g Protein; 267 mg Sodium

Pictured on page 35.

Honey Soy Halibut

Pale, tender fish covered in a sweet honey and soy sauce.

Liquid honey	3 tbsp.	50 mL
Soy sauce	3 tbsp.	50 mL
Grainy mustard	2 tbsp.	30 mL
Dried crushed chilies	1 tsp.	5 mL
Halibut steaks (about 6 oz., 170 g, each)	4	4

Combine first 4 ingredients in small bowl.

Preheat electric grill for 5 minutes or gas barbecue to medium-low. Brush both sides of each halibut steak with honey mixture. Cook on well-greased grill for 3 to 4 minutes per side (depending on thickness of steak) until fish flakes easily when tested with fork. Serves 4.

1 serving: 254 Calories; 4.5 g Total Fat (1.4 g Mono, 1.7 g Poly, 0.6 g Sat); 54 mg Cholesterol; 15 g Carbohydrate; trace Fibre; 37 g Protein; 987 mg Sodium

Paré Pointer
Forbidden fruit always makes a bad jam.

Shrimp On Sole

Casual yet could be considered fine dining on the patio!

MUSHROOM SAUCE

Hard margarine (or butter)	2 tbsp.	30 mL
Sliced fresh brown (or white) mushrooms	1 cup	250 mL
Sliced green onion	1/4 cup	60 mL
Slivered red pepper, 2 inch (5 cm) pieces	1/4 cup	60 mL
Dry white (or alcohol-free) wine	1/2 cup	125 mL
Salt	1/4 tsp.	1 mL
Granulated sugar	1/4 tsp.	1 mL
Water	2 tbsp.	30 mL
Cornstarch	1 tbsp.	15 mL
Sole fillets (about 4 oz., 113 g, each)	4	4
Raw medium shrimp (about 3 1/2 oz., 99 g), peeled, deveined, with or without tails left intact	12	12
Chopped fresh parsley (or 1 tsp., 5 mL, flakes)	4 tsp.	20 mL

Mushroom Sauce: Melt margarine in medium frying pan until sizzling. Sauté mushrooms on medium-high for 3 to 4 minutes until starting to brown. Add green onion and red pepper. Sauté for 1 to 2 minutes until soft.

Add wine, salt and sugar. Bring to a boil.

Stir water into cornstarch in small cup. Stir into mushroom mixture. Heat and stir until boiling and slightly thickened. Remove from heat. Makes 1 1/2 cups (375 mL) sauce.

Lay 1 sole fillet on 15 inch (38 cm) sheet of greased heavy-duty (or double layer of regular) foil. Arrange 3 shrimp on top. Spoon 2 to 3 tbsp. (30 to 50 mL) sauce over shrimp.

Sprinkle with 1 tsp. (5 mL) parsley. Wrap securely. Repeat to make 4 packets. Preheat gas barbecue to medium-high. Place packets on ungreased grill. Close lid. Cook for about 10 minutes, turning several times, until fish flakes easily when tested with fork and shrimp are pink and curled. Serves 4.

1 serving: 213 Calories; 7.6 g Total Fat (4.1 g Mono, 1.1 g Poly, 1.6 g Sat); 82 mg Cholesterol; 5 g Carbohydrate; 1 g Fibre; 26 g Protein; 339 mg Sodium

Pictured on page 143.

Halibut Steaks

Tender, moist halibut is enhanced by a mild citrus flavour.
Good with either lime or lemon.

Plain yogurt (not non-fat)	1/2 cup	125 mL
Lime (or lemon) juice	2 tbsp.	30 mL
Grated onion	2 tbsp.	30 mL
Halibut (or haddock) steaks (about 6 oz., 170 g, each)	4	4
Lime (or lemon), sliced lengthwise into quarters	1	1

Stir yogurt, lime juice and onion in small bowl.

Brush halibut steaks with yogurt mixture. Let stand on plate for 30 minutes. Preheat electric grill for 5 minutes. Cook halibut on greased grill for 7 to 9 minutes per side until fish flakes easily when tested with fork.

Grill lime, cut side down, until dark brown but not blackened. Squeeze over fish steaks when serving. Serves 4.

1 serving: 216 Calories; 4.4 g Total Fat (1.4 g Mono, 1.5 g Poly, 0.9 g Sat); 56 mg Cholesterol; 5 g Carbohydrate; trace Fibre; 37 g Protein; 115 mg Sodium

Barbecue Variation: Preheat gas barbecue to medium. Place halibut steaks on greased grill. Close lid. Cook for about 5 minutes per side until fish flakes easily when tested with fork.

Paré Pointer

Pulling a few strings from time to time really helps you get ahead, especially if you're a puppeteer.

Lemon Dill Bass

Sea bass is delicate, so be careful when turning.
The mild lemon and fresh dill subtly flavour the moist fish.

Lemon juice	1/4 cup	60 mL
Finely grated lemon zest	2 tsp.	10 mL
Chopped fresh dill (or 1 1/4 tsp., 6 mL, dill weed)	1 1/2 tbsp.	25 mL
Chopped fresh chives (or 3/4 tsp., 4 mL, dried)	1 tbsp.	15 mL
Paprika	1 tsp.	5 mL
Salt	1/2 tsp.	2 mL
Olive (or cooking) oil	2 tbsp.	30 mL
Fresh (or frozen, thawed) sea bass steak(s)	1 1/4 lbs.	560 g

Combine first 7 ingredients in shallow dish or resealable freezer bag.

Add fish. Turn to coat. Cover or seal. Marinate in refrigerator for 30 minutes. Drain and discard marinade. Preheat electric grill for 5 minutes or gas barbecue to medium. Cook fish on greased grill for 15 to 20 minutes, turning carefully after 10 minutes, until fish flakes easily when tested with fork. Divide into 4 portions, discarding bones and skin before serving. Serves 4.

1 serving: 169 Calories; 6.3 g Total Fat (3.1 g Mono, 1.4 g Poly, 1.2 g Sat); 57 mg Cholesterol; 1 g Carbohydrate; trace Fibre; 26 g Protein; 244 mg Sodium

1. Kefta Wraps, page 74
2. Indian Naan Bread, page 24

Props Courtesy Of: Island Pottery Inc.
Stokes

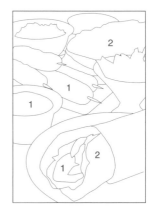

Mayonnaise Grilled Shrimp

Shiny, elegant-looking skewers that are very easy to make.
The flavoured mayonnaise has a fresh hint of lemon.

DRESSING

Mayonnaise (not salad dressing)	1/4 cup	60 mL
Garlic clove, minced (or 1/4 tsp., 1 mL, powder)	1	1
Lemon juice	1 tbsp.	15 mL
Chopped fresh parsley (or 3/4 tsp., 4 mL, flakes)	1 tbsp.	15 mL
Worcestershire sauce	1/2 tsp.	2 mL
Raw medium shrimp (about 1 1/2 lbs., 680 g), peeled, deveined and tails left intact	36	36
Bamboo skewers (8 inch, 20 cm, length), soaked in water for 10 minutes	6	6

Dressing: Stir first 5 ingredients in small bowl.

Thread 6 shrimp, all in same direction, onto each skewer. Preheat electric grill for 5 minutes or gas barbecue to medium. Cook shrimp on greased grill for about 4 minutes per side, brushing with generous dabs of dressing, until shrimp are firm and pink. Makes 6 skewers.

1 skewer: 174 Calories; 9.5 g Total Fat (4.6 g Mono, 3.3 g Poly, 1.1 g Sat); 150 mg Cholesterol; 1 g Carbohydrate; trace Fibre; 20 g Protein; 197 mg Sodium

1. Beer Bread, page 141
2. Beef And Chickpea Salad, page 92

Props Courtesy Of: Wiltshire ®

Beef And Chickpea Salad

A fresh, light, colourful salad with a mild curry flavour.

Mild curry paste	3 tbsp.	50 mL
Prepared orange juice	3 tbsp.	50 mL
Liquid honey	2 tbsp.	30 mL
Peanut (or cooking) oil	1 tbsp.	15 mL
Chili powder	1/2 tsp.	2 mL
Garlic salt	1/2 tsp.	2 mL
Rib-eye steak (about 6 oz., 170 g)	1	1
Fresh green beans, trimmed and halved	7 oz.	200 g
Boiling water		
Ice water		
Can of chickpeas, drained and rinsed	19 oz.	540 mL
Can of mandarin orange segments, drained	10 oz.	284 mL
Pistachios, shelled, skinned, toasted	1/2 cup	125 mL
(see Tip, page 146) and coarsely chopped		
Medium tomatoes, coarsely chopped	4	4
Lettuce leaves (your choice)		
DRESSING		
Olive (or cooking) oil	2 tbsp.	30 mL
Prepared orange juice	1 tbsp.	15 mL
White wine vinegar	1 tbsp.	15 mL
Dijon mustard	2 tsp.	10 mL
Salt	1/4 tsp.	1 mL

Combine first 6 ingredients in shallow dish or resealable freezer bag. Add steak. Turn to coat. Cover or seal. Marinate in refrigerator for at least 3 hours or overnight. Preheat electric grill for 5 minutes or gas barbecue to medium-high. Cook steak on greased grill for about 5 minutes per side until desired doneness. Cut across the grain into thin slices.

Cook beans in boiling water in medium saucepan for about 3 minutes until bright green and tender. Drain. Put into large bowl. Cover with ice water. Let stand for 10 minutes. Drain well.

Add steak and next 4 ingredients. Mix. Mound on lettuce on plates.

Dressing: Combine all 5 ingredients in jar with tight-fitting lid. Shake well. Makes 2/3 cup (150 mL) dressing. Drizzle over steak mixture. Toss. Makes about 8 1/2 cups (2.1 L).

1 cup (250 mL): 236 Calories; 13.7 g Total Fat (7.9 g Mono, 2.4 g Poly, 2.2 g Sat); 9 mg Cholesterol; 22 g Carbohydrate; 3 g Fibre; 9 g Protein; 243 mg Sodium

Pictured on page 90.

Chicken And Artichoke Salad

A colourful salad with a delicious blend of flavours and textures.

MARINADE/DRESSING

Garlic cloves, minced (or 1/2 tsp., 2 mL, powder)	2	2
Olive (or cooking) oil	1/3 cup	75 mL
Balsamic vinegar	1/4 cup	60 mL
Liquid honey	2 tbsp.	30 mL
Chopped fresh sweet basil (or 3/4 tsp., 4 mL, dried)	1 tbsp.	15 mL
Lemon pepper	1 tsp.	5 mL
Boneless, skinless chicken breast halves (about 3)	12 oz.	340 g
Large red onion, cut into 8 wedges	1	1
Bag of baby spinach leaves (or arugula)	6 oz.	170 g
Can of artichoke hearts, drained and coarsely chopped	14 oz.	398 mL
Crumbled feta cheese	3/4 cup	175 mL
Halved cherry tomatoes	1 cup	250 mL
Walnuts, toasted (see Tip, page 146) and chopped	1 cup	250 mL

Marinade/Dressing: Combine first 6 ingredients in jar with tight-fitting lid. Shake well. Makes 3/4 cup (175 mL) marinade.

Put 1/2 of marinade into shallow dish or resealable freezer bag. Add chicken. Turn to coat. Cover or seal. Marinate in refrigerator for 3 hours. Drain and discard marinade. Preheat electric grill for 5 minutes or gas barbecue to medium. Cook chicken on greased grill for about 5 minutes per side until no longer pink inside. Chop coarsely. Put into large bowl.

Cook red onion on greased grill for about 10 minutes, turning once, until browned. Add to chicken.

Add remaining 5 ingredients. Just before serving, drizzle with remaining dressing. Toss. Makes about 11 cups (2.75 L).

1 cup (250 mL): 232 Calories; 16.8 g Total Fat (7.3 g Mono, 5.3 g Poly, 3.2 g Sat); 28 mg Cholesterol; 10 g Carbohydrate; 2 g Fibre; 13 g Protein; 203 mg Sodium

Pictured on page 53.

Chicken Pita Salad

Chunky greens and crispy pitas tossed in a tangy dressing.

LEMON GARLIC DRESSING

Olive (or cooking) oil	1/4 cup	60 mL
Lemon juice	3 tbsp.	50 mL
Garlic clove, minced (or 1/4 tsp., 1 mL, powder)	1	1
Granulated sugar	1 tsp.	5 mL
Chili powder	1/4 tsp.	1 mL
Chopped fresh mint leaves (or 1 1/2 tsp., 7 mL, dried)	2 tbsp.	30 mL
Chopped fresh parsley (or 1 1/2 tsp., 7 mL, flakes)	2 tbsp.	30 mL
Ground cinnamon	1/4 tsp.	1 mL
Salt	1/4 tsp.	1 mL
Boneless, skinless chicken breast halves (about 2)	8 oz.	225 g
Small yellow (or green) zucchini, with peel, cut lengthwise into 1/4 inch (6 mm) thick slices	2	2
Pita breads (6 inch, 15 cm, diameter)	2	2
Baby salad greens (or mesclun mix)	4 cups	1 L
Pepitas (pumpkin seed kernels)	1/4 cup	60 mL
Crumbled feta cheese (about 1 1/2 oz., 43 g)	1/3 cup	75 mL

Lemon Garlic Dressing: Combine first 9 ingredients in jar with tight-fitting lid. Shake well. Makes 1/2 cup (125 mL) dressing.

Preheat electric grill for 5 minutes or gas barbecue to medium. Cook chicken on greased grill for about 5 minutes per side until no longer pink inside. Cut into 1/4 inch (6 mm) thick slices.

Cook zucchini on greased grill for about 3 minutes per side until tender-crisp. Cut into 1 1/2 inch (3.8 cm) pieces.

Place pitas on greased grill. Cook for 3 to 4 minutes per side until crisp. Cool. Break into 1 1/2 inch (3.8 cm) pieces.

Combine chicken, zucchini, pita and remaining 3 ingredients in large bowl. Drizzle with dressing. Toss. Makes about 8 cups (2 L).

1 cup (250 mL): 212 Calories; 12.7 g Total Fat (6.7 g Mono, 2.3 g Poly, 2.8 g Sat); 22 mg Cholesterol; 13 g Carbohydrate; 2 g Fibre; 12 g Protein; 246 mg Sodium

Pictured on front cover.

Veggie Pasta Salad

Grilled vegetables tossed with pasta in a creamy sun-dried tomato sauce. Delicious!

Roma (plum) tomatoes, cut in wedges	8	8
Olive (or cooking) oil	2 tbsp.	30 mL
Balsamic vinegar	2 tbsp.	30 mL
Garlic clove, chopped (or 1/4 tsp., 1 mL, powder)	1	1
Chopped green onion	1/2 cup	125 mL
Italian seasoning	1/2 tsp.	2 mL
Granulated sugar	1/2 tsp.	2 mL
Salt, sprinkle		
Pepper, sprinkle		
Large red peppers, quartered	2	2
Green zucchini, cut lengthwise into 1/4 inch (6 mm) thick slices	2	2
Small eggplant, cut lengthwise into 1/4 inch (6 mm) thick slices	1	1
Cooked penne pasta, cooled (about 2 cups, 500 mL, uncooked)	4 cups	1 L
Sour cream	1/3 cup	75 mL
Sun-dried tomato pesto	1/4 cup	60 mL

Combine first 9 ingredients in medium bowl. Transfer to medium foil pan. Preheat gas barbecue to medium-high. Place pan on ungreased grill. Close lid. Grill for about 15 minutes, stirring occasionally, until tomato is soft. Remove tomato to large bowl. Discard liquid.

Cook red peppers on greased grill for about 15 minutes, turning occasionally, until grill marks appear and skins are slightly blackened. Chop coarsely. Add to tomato.

Cook zucchini and eggplant slices on greased grill for 3 to 4 minutes per side until browned. Chop coarsely. Add to tomato mixture.

Add pasta. Toss.

Combine sour cream and pesto in small bowl. Add to pasta mixture. Toss to coat. Makes about 10 cups (2.5 L).

1 cup (250 mL): 174 Calories; 5.2 g Total Fat (2.7 g Mono, 0.7 g Poly, 1.3 g Sat); 3 mg Cholesterol; 29 g Carbohydrate; 3 g Fibre; 5 g Protein; 48 mg Sodium

Beef Fajita Salad

Enjoy the great taste of a fajita in a salad!
Serve with sour cream, salsa and guacamole.

Lime juice	1/2 cup	125 mL
Garlic cloves (or 1 tsp., 5 mL, powder)	4	4
Coarsely chopped onion	1/3 cup	75 mL
Ground cumin	1 1/2 tsp.	7 mL
Pepper	1/2 tsp.	2 mL
Cayenne pepper	1/4 tsp.	1 mL
Chili powder	1/4 tsp.	1 mL
Top sirloin steak	12 oz.	340 g
Cooking oil	2 tbsp.	30 mL
Medium red pepper, slivered lengthwise	1	1
Medium yellow pepper, slivered lengthwise	1	1
Large onion, sliced lengthwise	1	1
Large flour tortillas (10 inch, 25 cm, diameter), your choice	3	3
Crisp torn lettuce (such as iceberg or romaine), lightly packed	8 cups	2 L
Salt, sprinkle		
Pepper, sprinkle		
Grated sharp Cheddar cheese	1/2 cup	125 mL
Green onions, sliced	2	2
Medium tomatoes, seeded and diced	2	2
Sour cream (optional)	1/2 cup	125 mL

Process first 7 ingredients in blender until smooth. Pour about 1/3 cup (75 mL) into shallow dish or resealable freezer bag. Reserve remaining marinade.

Add steak to dish or bag. Turn to coat. Cover or seal. Marinate at room temperature for 30 minutes, turning once. Drain and discard marinade. Preheat gas barbecue to high. Sear steak on greased grill, with lid open, for 1 minute per side. Cook for about 3 minutes per side until medium-rare or until desired doneness. Remove to cutting board. Tent with foil for 10 minutes. Cut diagonally across the grain into 1/8 inch (3 mm) thick slices. Turn into large bowl with any accumulated juices.

(continued on next page)

Meal Salads

Add cooking oil to reserved marinade. Pour into 9 × 13 inch (22 × 33 cm) metal or foil pan. Add peppers and onion. Toss well. Place pan on grill. Cook, with lid open, for about 10 minutes, stirring occasionally, until vegetables are tender-crisp. Add to beef, along with any liquid from pan. Toss.

Place tortillas on grill. Cook, with lid open, turning several times, until browned and crisp. Place on plate to cool slightly. Break each into 4 large pieces.

Arrange lettuce on 4 large plates. Divide beef mixture over lettuce, spooning any accumulated liquid over top. Sprinkle with salt and pepper.

Divide and sprinkle cheese, green onion and tomato over top. Serve with tortillas.

Serve with sour cream. Serves 4.

1 serving: 464 Calories; 21.5 g Total Fat (9.2 g Mono, 4 g Poly, 6.4 g Sat); 53 mg Cholesterol; 45 g Carbohydrate; 4 g Fibre; 25 g Protein; 358 mg Sodium

Pictured on page 107.

 tip   *Grilling times for vegetables may vary. Softer vegetables, such as tomatoes and mushrooms, take very little time to cook, whereas potatoes, beets and other root vegetables may need to be blanched or boiled beforehand to cut down on grilling time and prevent burning. If you are mixing vegetables in a packet or on a skewer, select those with similar texture so that the contents cook evenly.*

Pizza Patty Supper Loaf

The spicy cheese filling oozes out of this well-browned meatloaf.
A filling meal when served with mashed potatoes and salad.

Fine dry bread crumbs	1/2 cup	125 mL
Seasoned salt	1/2 tsp.	2 mL
Onion powder	1/2 tsp.	2 mL
Ground whole oregano	1/4 tsp.	1 mL
Ground thyme	1/4 tsp.	1 mL
Garlic powder	1/4 tsp.	1 mL
Cayenne pepper	1/8 tsp.	0.5 mL
Lean ground beef	1/2 lb.	225 g
Lean ground pork	1/2 lb.	225 g
Large egg, fork-beaten	1	1
FILLING		
Grated mozzarella cheese	3 tbsp.	50 mL
Grated Asiago (or mozzarella) cheese	2 tbsp.	30 mL
Chopped fresh mushrooms	1 tbsp.	15 mL
Finely diced green (or red) pepper	1 tbsp.	15 mL
Grated Parmesan cheese	1 tbsp.	15 mL
Green onion, thinly sliced	1	1
Chunky salsa	3 tbsp.	50 mL
All-purpose flour	1 tsp.	5 mL

Stir first 7 ingredients in large bowl.

Add ground beef, ground pork and egg. Stir well to combine. Divide into 2 equal portions. Place 1 portion on 10 inch (25 cm) sheet of foil or waxed paper. Pat out into even layer, about 1/2 inch (12 mm) thick, slightly smaller in width and length than your two-sided grill.

Filling: Stir first 7 ingredients in small bowl. Turn out onto meat mixture. Spread filling to within 1/2 inch (12 mm) of all edges.

Sprinkle flour on uncovered edges. Flatten remaining meat mixture to same size. Place over top of filling. Press and mold edges to seal well. Preheat lightly greased two-sided grill for 5 minutes. Place meatloaf on grill. Peel off foil and discard. Close lid. Cook for about 15 minutes until meat is no longer pink inside and cheese is melted. Let meatloaf rest on grill, with lid open, for about 10 minutes until firm. Serves 4.

1 serving: 264 Calories; 12.3 g Total Fat (5 g Mono, 0.9 g Poly, 5.1 g Sat); 114 mg Cholesterol; 13 g Carbohydrate; 1 g Fibre; 25 g Protein; 421 mg Sodium

Stuffed Portobello Entree

*Serve these exotic-flavoured mushrooms with rice
or couscous to absorb the delicious juices.*

Portobello mushrooms (4 inch, 10 cm, diameter)	4	4
Fine dry bread crumbs	4 tsp.	20 mL
Lean ground pork	1/2 lb.	225 g
Oyster sauce	2 tbsp.	30 mL
Parsley flakes	2 tsp.	10 mL
Garlic powder	1/2 tsp.	2 mL
Onion powder	1/2 tsp.	2 mL
Ground ginger	1/4 tsp.	1 mL
Cayenne pepper	1/4 tsp.	1 mL
Whole onion slices, 1/4 inch (6 mm) thick	4	4
Sesame (or cooking) oil	2 tsp.	10 mL

Scrape away and discard black gills from inside mushrooms. Sprinkle cavity of each with 1 tsp. (5 mL) bread crumbs.

Combine next 7 ingredients in small bowl. Divide and evenly pack into mushroom cavities.

Place onion slice on top of pork mixture on each mushroom. Brush onion with sesame oil. Preheat lightly greased two-sided grill for 5 minutes. Place mushrooms, stuffing-side up, on grill. Close lid. Cook for about 8 minutes until mushrooms are tender and pork is no longer pink inside. Makes 4 stuffed mushrooms.

1 stuffed mushroom: 131 Calories; 5.8 g Total Fat (2.3 g Mono, 1.4 g Poly, 1.5 g Sat); 23 mg Cholesterol; 10 g Carbohydrate; 1 g Fibre; 11 g Protein; 785 mg Sodium

Pictured on page 126.

Paré Pointer

He races pigeons but he has never beat them.

Grilled Ratatouille Salsa

A zesty side dish that can also be served bruschetta-style on fresh bread slices.
Serve at room temperature for the best flavour.

LEMON MUSTARD DRESSING

Olive (or cooking) oil	3 tbsp.	50 mL
Lemon juice	2 tbsp.	30 mL
Grainy mustard	1 tbsp.	15 mL
Worcestershire sauce	2 tsp.	10 mL
Granulated sugar	1/2 tsp.	2 mL
Finely grated lemon zest	1/4 tsp.	1 mL
Garlic clove, minced (or 1/4 tsp., 1 mL, powder)	1	1
Finely chopped fresh sweet basil (or 3/4 tsp., 4 mL, dried)	1 tbsp.	15 mL
Finely chopped fresh parsley (or 3/4 tsp., 4 mL, flakes)	1 tbsp.	15 mL
Salt	1/2 tsp.	2 mL
Pepper, heavy sprinkle		
Large red onion, peeled and cut in half crosswise	1	1
Asian eggplant, with peel, cut in half lengthwise (or small globe eggplant, cut crosswise into 1 1/2 inch, 3.8 cm, slices)	1	1
Roma (plum) tomatoes, diced	3	3
Shredded fresh spinach leaves, packed	1 cup	250 mL
Sliced ripe olives	3 tbsp.	50 mL

Lemon Mustard Dressing: Combine first 11 ingredients in large bowl. Reserve 1 tbsp. (15 mL) in small cup.

Generously brush cut sides of red onion and eggplant with reserved dressing. Preheat lightly greased two-sided grill for 5 minutes. Place onion and eggplant, cut sides down, in single layer on grill. Close lid. Cook for about 10 minutes until onion is tender-crisp and eggplant is soft. Remove to cutting board. Dice into 1/2 inch (12 mm) pieces. Add to dressing. Toss to coat.

(continued on next page)

Add tomato, spinach and olives. Toss. Makes about 5 cups (1.25 L). Serves 6 as a side dish.

1 serving: 116 Calories; 7.8 g Total Fat (5.4 g Mono, 0.9 g Poly, 1.1 g Sat); 0 mg Cholesterol; 11 g Carbohydrate; 2 g Fibre; 2 g Protein; 295 mg Sodium

Pictured on page 36.

Mediterranean Rolls

Crusty ciabatta rolls that are stuffed with colourful, fresh ingredients.
The tang of the lemon-flavoured mayonnaise adds a special touch.

Small zucchini, with peel, thinly sliced lengthwise	2	2
Olive (or cooking) oil		
Salt, sprinkle		
Mayonnaise (not salad dressing)	1/3 cup	75 mL
Finely grated lemon zest	1/4 tsp.	1 mL
Lemon juice	1 tbsp.	15 mL
Granulated sugar	1/2 tsp.	2 mL
Ciabatta rolls (or your choice), cut in half	4	4
Jar of artichoke hearts, drained and coarsely chopped	6 oz.	170 mL
Roma (plum) tomatoes, sliced	2	2
Salami slices (about 2 1/2 oz., 70 g)	12	12
Mozzarella cheese slices	8	8

Brush both sides of each zucchini slice with olive oil. Sprinkle with salt. Preheat lightly greased two-sided grill for 5 minutes. Place zucchini on grill. Close lid. Cook for 5 to 8 minutes until tender-crisp.

Combine next 4 ingredients in small bowl. Spread cut sides of each roll with mayonnaise mixture.

Divide and layer zucchini and remaining 4 ingredients on bottom halves of rolls. Cover with top halves. Place on grill. Close lid. Cook for about 10 minutes until rolls are crisp. Makes 4 sandwiches.

1 sandwich: 558 Calories; 39.6 g Total Fat (18.5 g Mono, 6.9 g Poly, 12.5 g Sat); 75 mg Cholesterol; 30 g Carbohydrate; 3 g Fibre; 22 g Protein; 965 mg Sodium

Pictured on page 108 and on back cover.

Sweet Pineapple Burgers

The appealing flavours of Asiago cheese, pineapple and green pepper combine in these big, juicy patties. Jalapeño pepper jelly is optional, but the wonderful flavour it creates makes it worth hunting for!

Lean ground beef	1 lb.	454 g
Evaporated milk	1/3 cup	75 mL
Large egg, fork-beaten	1	1
Fresh bread crumbs	1 cup	250 mL
Finely chopped green pepper	1/2 cup	125 mL
Green onion, thinly sliced	1	1
Garlic clove, minced (or 1/4 tsp., 1 mL, powder), optional	1	1
Salt	3/4 tsp.	4 mL
Pepper	1/8 tsp.	0.5 mL
Cayenne pepper	1/8 tsp.	0.5 mL
Canned pineapple slices, drained	8	8
Asiago (or mozzarella) cheese, thinly sliced	4 oz.	113 g
Jalapeño pepper jelly (optional)	3 tbsp.	50 mL
Salad dressing (or mayonnaise)	3 tbsp.	50 mL
Prepared mustard	1 tbsp.	15 mL
Kaiser rolls (or large hamburger buns), cut in half and toasted (buttered, optional)	4	4
Lettuce leaves (your choice)	4	4

Mix first 10 ingredients in large bowl. Divide and shape into four 4 inch (10 cm) patties. Preheat lightly greased two-sided grill for 5 minutes.

Place 4 pineapple slices on grill. Lay patties on top of pineapple. Place remaining pineapple slices on top of patties. Close lid. Cook for about 10 minutes until patties are no longer pink inside.

Divide and layer cheese on top of pineapple. Let stand on grill, with lid open, for about 3 minutes until cheese is melted.

Divide and spread jelly, salad dressing and mustard on cut sides of rolls. Layer patties and lettuce leaves on bottom halves. Cover with top halves. Makes 4 burgers.

1 burger: 690 Calories; 29 g Total Fat (11.5 g Mono, 4.3 g Poly, 10.3 g Sat); 143 mg Cholesterol; 67 g Carbohydrate; 3 g Fibre; 39 g Protein; 1333 mg Sodium

Pictured on page 125.

Apple French Toasts

These thick, apple-topped toasts are delicious
with maple (or maple-flavoured) syrup.

Large eggs	3	3
Milk	1 cup	250 mL
Brown sugar, packed	3 tbsp.	50 mL
Vanilla	1 tsp.	5 mL
Ground cinnamon	1/2 tsp.	2 mL
Salt	1/4 tsp.	1 mL
Slices of multi-grain bread (about 1 1/4 inches, 3 cm, thick)	4	4
Medium cooking apples (such as McIntosh), peeled, cored and thinly sliced	2	2
Hard margarine (or butter), melted	2 tbsp.	30 mL
Icing (confectioner's) sugar	1 tbsp.	15 mL
Ground cinnamon	1/4 tsp.	1 mL

Beat first 6 ingredients in medium bowl until smooth.

Place bread in pan large enough to hold in single layer. Pour egg mixture over bread. Turn. Let stand for about 5 minutes until liquid is absorbed.

Preheat lightly greased two-sided grill for 5 minutes. Remove bread from pan. Place bread on grill. Lay apple on top of bread to cover well. Drizzle about 1 1/2 tsp. (7 mL) margarine over each. Close lid. Cook for about 8 minutes until apple is tender and toast is firm.

Stir icing sugar and second amount of cinnamon in small dish. Sprinkle over hot toast. Serves 4.

1 serving: 382 Calories; 12.9 g Total Fat (6.4 g Mono, 1.8 g Poly, 3.3 g Sat); 164 mg Cholesterol; 55 g Carbohydrate; 6 g Fibre; 13 g Protein; 612 mg Sodium

Paré Pointer

A car is a car and then it turns into a driveway.

Sweet Orange Salmon

A quick, easy-to-make recipe that is perfect for entertaining.
The fresh, tasty Orange Butter is the perfect addition to the salmon.

Prepared orange juice	1/2 cup	125 mL
Brown sugar, packed	3 tbsp.	50 mL
Peanut (or cooking) oil	2 tbsp.	30 mL
Soy sauce	2 tbsp.	30 mL
Garlic cloves, minced (or 1/2 tsp., 2 mL, powder)	2	2
Centre-cut salmon fillets (about 4 oz., 113 g, each), skin removed	4	4
ORANGE BUTTER		
Bacon slices, finely chopped	2	2
Butter (or hard margarine), softened	1/3 cup	75 mL
Chopped fresh parsley (or 3/4 tsp., 4 mL, flakes)	1 tbsp.	15 mL
Orange marmalade	2 tbsp.	30 mL
Coarsely ground pepper (or 1/4 tsp., 1 mL, pepper)	1/2 tsp.	2 mL

Combine first 5 ingredients in shallow dish or resealable freezer bag.

Add salmon. Turn to coat. Cover or seal. Marinate in refrigerator for at least 6 hours or overnight.

Orange Butter: Cook bacon in small frying pan on medium for about 5 minutes until crisp. Drain on paper towel. Cool. Put into small bowl.

Add remaining 4 ingredients. Mix well. Shape butter mixture into 4 inch (10 cm) log on sheet of waxed paper. Wrap with waxed paper. Chill for 1 to 2 hours until firm. Cut into eight 1/2 inch (12 mm) thick rounds. Preheat well-greased two-sided grill for 5 minutes. Drain and discard marinade. Place salmon on grill. Close lid. Cook for about 5 minutes until salmon flakes easily when tested with fork. Top each piece of salmon with 2 slices of butter mixture. Serves 4.

1 serving: 455 Calories; 33.4 g Total Fat (11.4 g Mono, 6.3 g Poly, 13.7 g Sat); 113 mg Cholesterol; 14 g Carbohydrate; trace Fibre; 24 g Protein; 551 mg Sodium

Pictured on page 71.

Pork Pitas

Fun, casual pitas stuffed with tomato, onion and pork. Grilling the
marinated pork pieces on skewers makes them easier and faster to turn.

Olive (or cooking) oil	2 tbsp.	30 mL
Lemon juice	2 tbsp.	30 mL
Liquid honey	2 tbsp.	30 mL
Lemon pepper	1 tbsp.	15 mL
Chili powder	1/2 tsp.	2 mL
Garlic powder	1/2 tsp.	2 mL
Dried oregano	1/2 tsp.	2 mL
Pork tenderloin, cut into 3/4 inch (2 cm) cubes	3/4 lb.	340 g
Bamboo skewers (8 inch, 20 cm, length), soaked in water for 10 minutes	4	4
Plain yogurt	2/3 cup	150 mL
Chopped fresh parsley (or 1 1/2 tsp., 7 mL, flakes)	2 tbsp.	30 mL
Pita breads (7 inch, 18 cm, diameter)	4	4
Medium tomatoes, thinly sliced	2	2
Slivered red onion	2/3 cup	150 mL

Combine first 7 ingredients in large bowl or resealable freezer bag.

Add pork. Stir to coat. Cover or seal. Marinate in refrigerator for at least 3 hours or overnight. Drain and discard marinade.

Thread pork onto skewers. Preheat lightly greased two-sided grill for 5 minutes. Place skewers on grill. Close lid. Cook for about 10 minutes, turning once, until tender. Remove pork from skewers.

Combine yogurt and parsley in small bowl. Divide and spread over pitas.

Place pork, tomato and red onion down centre of pitas. Fold over to cover filling. Makes 4 pitas.

1 pita: 375 Calories; 7.5 g Total Fat (3.8 g Mono, 1 g Poly, 1.9 g Sat); 48 mg Cholesterol;
47 g Carbohydrate; 2 g Fibre; 29 g Protein; 399 mg Sodium

Super-Seasoned Spuds

Well-seasoned, crispy potatoes with a nice grilled appearance.

Medium potatoes, cut lengthwise into 8 wedges each	2	2
Olive (or cooking) oil	1 tbsp.	15 mL
Seasoned salt	3/4 tsp.	4 mL
Granulated sugar	1/2 tsp.	2 mL
Paprika	1/2 tsp.	2 mL
Dry mustard	1/4 tsp.	1 mL
Garlic powder	1/4 tsp.	1 mL
Chili powder	1/4 tsp.	1 mL
Cayenne pepper	1/8 tsp.	0.5 mL
Coarsely ground pepper, heavy sprinkle		

Toss potato in olive oil in medium bowl until coated.

Combine next 8 ingredients in small cup. Sprinkle over potato. Stir well to coat. Preheat lightly greased two-sided grill for 5 minutes. Place potato in even layer on grill. Spoon any olive oil mixture from bowl over potato. Close lid. Cook for about 20 minutes until potato is crispy and grilled. Makes 16 wedges. Serves 2 to 3.

1 serving: 182 Calories; 7.3 g Total Fat (5.1 g Mono, 0.7 g Poly, 1 g Sat); 0 mg Cholesterol; 27 g Carbohydrate; 3 g Fibre; 4 g Protein; 459 mg Sodium

Pictured on page 125.

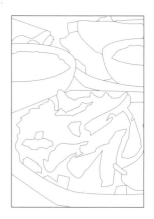

Beef Fajita Salad, page 96

Props Courtesy Of: Zenari's

Steak And Mushrooms

The hot, spicy steak and sweet mushrooms are a nice combination.
A delicious dish for two.

Coarsely ground pepper	1 tsp.	5 mL
Cajun seasoning	1 tsp.	5 mL
Garlic salt	1/2 tsp.	2 mL
Rib-eye steaks (about 4 oz., 113 g, each)	2	2
Olive (or cooking) oil	1 tbsp.	15 mL
Honey mustard	1 tbsp.	15 mL
Crushed dried rosemary	1/4 tsp.	1 mL
Fresh medium mushrooms, stems removed	8	8

Combine first 3 ingredients in small cup.

Sprinkle over both sides of each steak. Preheat lightly greased two-sided grill for 5 minutes. Place steaks on grill. Cook for 5 to 7 minutes until desired doneness.

Combine olive oil, mustard and rosemary in medium bowl. Add mushrooms. Toss to coat. Place mushrooms on grill. Close lid. Cook for 4 to 5 minutes until tender. Serve with steak. Serves 2.

1 serving: 282 Calories; 17.1 g Total Fat (9.2 g Mono, 1.2 g Poly, 4.9 g Sat); 51 mg Cholesterol; 9 g Carbohydrate; 1 g Fibre; 23 g Protein; 793 mg Sodium

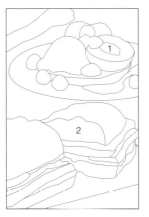

1. Balsamic Peaches, page 136
2. Mediterranean Rolls, page 101

Props Courtesy Of: Casa Bugatti
The Bay

Wood Chips & Other Aromatics

Adding mesquite, hickory, maple, fruitwood or other aromatic wood chips to the barbecue imparts a delicious, wood-smoked flavour that makes grilled food taste so unique.

Bags of wood chips can be purchased at most stores that sell barbecue equipment. Wood chips require soaking for at least 15 minutes, and up to 30 minutes, depending on their size and the length of time they will be smoking.

The best container for the chips is a cast-iron smoker box, available for a reasonable price at most stores that sell barbecue equipment. However, you can make your own container using heavy-duty foil or foil pans that have had holes poked in the top. The chips (a combination of wet and dry) are put into the container and the container is then set either directly on the heat source or on the grill over the heat source. If cooking time is much longer than 30 minutes, the wood chips should be farther away from the heat to ensure they continue to smoke for length of time required. Avoid lifting lid of the barbecue during the cooking time, except for turning or basting the food, for maximum smoke flavour.

Dried herbs are another great aromatic. Select a combination of your favourite dried herbs, soak in water, squeeze out excess moisture, and then sprinkle in a foil pan and place directly on the heat source. For a really quick aromatic, put citrus peel or fresh rosemary sprigs into a foil pan and place directly on heat source.

Smoked Eggplant Dip

Serve as an appetizer with crispy pita chips or Indian Naan Bread, page 24. This is so delicious you may want to double the recipe.

Mesquite (or hickory) wood chips	1 cup	250 mL
Water		
Medium eggplant, with peel, halved lengthwise	1	1
Olive (or cooking) oil	2 tbsp.	30 mL

(continued on next page)

Whole wheat bread slices, crusts removed and bread torn into small pieces	2	2
Olive (or cooking) oil	1 tbsp.	15 mL
Lemon juice	2 tsp.	10 mL
Garlic clove (or 1/4 tsp., 1 mL, powder)	1	1
Paprika	1/2 tsp.	2 mL
Salt	1/4 tsp.	1 mL
Pepper, sprinkle		

Put 1/2 of dry wood chips into smoker box. Soak remaining chips in water in small bowl for 15 to 30 minutes. Drain. Place on top of dry chips. Close smoker box. Remove 1 side of grill from gas barbecue. Place smoker box directly on heat source. Replace grill. Close lid. Heat barbecue to medium for 15 to 20 minutes until chips are smoking. Adjust burner under smoker box as necessary to keep it smoking. Adjust opposite burner to maintain medium-low barbecue temperature.

Brush cut sides of eggplant with first amount of olive oil. Place eggplant, cut side up, on greased grill directly over smoker box. Cook for 10 minutes. Turn eggplant. Cook for about 5 minutes until soft.

Put bread into food processor. Process until coarse crumbs. Scrape eggplant from skin. Add eggplant to bread crumbs.

Add next 6 ingredients. Process until smooth. Serve warm or cold. Makes 1 2/3 cups (400 mL).

2 tbsp. (30 mL): 42 Calories; 2.8 g Total Fat (2 g Mono, 0.2 g Poly, 0.4 g Sat); 0 mg Cholesterol; 4 g Carbohydrate; trace Fibre; 1 g Protein; 66 mg Sodium

 To douse flames if wood chips catch on fire, keep a spray bottle of water handy. Dousing will also cause more smoke to form, which is preferable to charring. Ideally, the chips should be kept just below "burning" for smoke to be maintained.

Spicy Surf 'N' Turf

These well-seasoned skewers are sure to become a favourite.
Adjust the Cajun seasoning as desired.

Worcestershire sauce	2 tbsp.	30 mL
Cajun seasoning	2 tbsp.	30 mL
Olive (or cooking) oil	1 tbsp.	15 mL
Brown sugar, packed	1 tbsp.	15 mL
Chopped fresh parsley (or 3/4 tsp., 7 mL, flakes)	1 tbsp.	15 mL
Garlic cloves, minced (or 1/2 tsp., 2 mL, powder)	2	2
Salt	1/2 tsp.	2 mL
Beef tenderloin, cut into 3/4 inch (2 cm) cubes (about 24)	10 oz.	285 g
Raw large shrimp, tails intact (about 24), peeled and deveined	10 oz.	285 g
Mesquite (or hickory) wood chips	1 cup	250 mL
Water		
Bamboo skewers (12 inch, 30 cm, length), soaked in water for 10 minutes	8	8

Combine first 7 ingredients in large bowl or resealable freezer bag.

Add beef and shrimp. Stir to coat. Cover or seal. Marinate in refrigerator for 1 to 3 hours.

Put 1/2 of dry wood chips into smoker box. Soak remaining chips in water in small bowl for 15 to 30 minutes. Drain. Place on top of dry chips. Close smoker box. Remove 1 side of grill from gas barbecue. Place smoker box directly on heat source. Replace grill. Close lid. Heat barbecue to medium for 15 to 20 minutes until chips are smoking. Adjust burner under smoker box as necessary to keep it smoking. Adjust opposite burner to maintain medium barbecue temperature.

Thread beef and shrimp alternately onto skewers. Place skewers on greased grill directly over smoker box. Cook for 5 to 7 minutes, turning occasionally, until beef is tender and shrimp are pink and curled. Makes 8 skewers.

1 skewer: 107 Calories; 4.2 g Total Fat (2 g Mono, 0.5 g Poly, 1 g Sat); 68 mg Cholesterol; 3 g Carbohydrate; trace Fibre; 13 g Protein; 861 mg Sodium

Country-Style Pork

Moist, tender pork with a golden glaze. You'll love the
wonderful smoky taste that permeates the meat.

MARINADE

Barbecue sauce (mesquite or hickory flavour is best)	1 cup	250 mL
Liquid honey	1/4 cup	60 mL
Soy sauce	1 tbsp.	15 mL
Chopped onion	1/2 cup	125 mL
Garlic cloves, minced (or 1/2 tsp., 2 mL, powder), optional	2	2
Country-style pork rib ends	3 lbs.	1.4 kg
Mesquite (or hickory) wood chips	1 1/2 cups	375 mL
Water		

Marinade: Combine first 5 ingredients in small bowl. Makes 1 2/3 cups (400 mL) marinade. Pour into shallow dish or resealable freezer bag.

Add ribs. Turn to coat. Cover or seal. Marinate in refrigerator for at least 4 hours or up to 24 hours, turning several times.

Put 1/2 of dry wood chips into smoker box. Soak remaining chips in water in medium bowl for 15 to 30 minutes. Drain. Place on top of dry chips. Close smoker box. Place on grill on 1 side of gas barbecue. Close lid. Heat barbecue to medium for 15 to 20 minutes until chips are smoking. Adjust burner under smoker box as necessary to keep it smoking. Adjust opposite burner to maintain medium-low barbecue temperature. Remove grill opposite smoker box using oven mitts. Place drip pan, with 1 inch (2.5 cm) water, directly on heat source. Replace grill. Drain and discard marinade. Arrange ribs on greased grill over drip pan. Close lid. Cook for 1 hour. Turn ribs. Replenish water in pan if necessary. Cook ribs for 15 to 20 minutes until tender and glazed. Serves 6.

1 serving: 437 Calories; 31 g Total Fat (13.5 g Mono, 2.6 g Poly, 11.2 g Sat); 111 mg Cholesterol; 9 g Carbohydrate; 1 g Fibre; 29 g Protein; 330 mg Sodium

Dry Curry Ribs

Tender ribs with a delicate curry flavour on the outside
and moist meat on the inside.

CURRY RUB

Curry powder	2 tbsp.	30 mL
Cajun seasoning	2 tbsp.	30 mL
Brown sugar, packed	2 tbsp.	30 mL
Lemon pepper	2 tbsp.	30 mL
Dried oregano	1 tbsp.	15 mL
Garlic salt	2 tsp.	10 mL
Finely grated orange zest	1 tsp.	5 mL
Pork side ribs, cut into 4 portions	3 lbs.	1.4 kg
Maple wood chips	1 1/2 cups	375 mL
Water		

Curry Rub: Combine first 7 ingredients in small bowl. Makes 2/3 cup (150 mL) rub.

Rub mixture over both sides of each portion of ribs. Place in shallow dish, on baking sheet or on platter. Cover. Marinate in refrigerator for at least 6 hours or overnight.

Put 1/2 of dry wood chips into smoker box. Soak remaining chips in water in medium bowl for 15 to 30 minutes. Drain. Place on top of dry chips. Close smoker box. Place on grill on 1 side of gas barbecue. Close lid. Heat barbecue to medium for 15 to 20 minutes until chips are smoking. Turn off burner opposite smoker box. Turn burner under smoker box to medium. Place ribs on greased grill on unlit side. Close lid. Cook for 1 to 1 1/2 hours, turning occasionally, until tender. Serves 4.

1 serving: 672 Calories; 46.6 g Total Fat (19.8 g Mono, 4.3 g Poly, 17.3 g Sat); 175 mg Cholesterol; 13 g Carbohydrate; 2 g Fibre; 49 g Protein; 1990 mg Sodium

Pictured on page 53.

Screaming Hot Wings

For those who don't like too much "heat" in their food,
try the milder variation below.

Peach (or apricot) nectar	1 cup	250 mL
Barbecue sauce	1/2 cup	125 mL
Ketchup	1/4 cup	60 mL
White wine vinegar	1/4 cup	60 mL
Hot pepper sauce	1 – 2 tbsp.	15 – 30 mL
Garlic powder	2 tsp.	10 mL
Celery salt	2 tsp.	10 mL
Whole chicken wings, split in half and tips discarded (or drumettes)	3 lbs.	1.4 kg
Mesquite (or hickory) wood chips	1 1/2 cups	375 mL
Water		

Combine first 7 ingredients in large bowl or resealable freezer bag. Makes about 2 cups (500 mL) marinade.

Add chicken. Stir to coat. Cover or seal. Marinate in refrigerator for at least 8 hours or overnight. Drain, reserving marinade. Boil marinade in small saucepan for 5 minutes.

Put 1/2 of dry wood chips into smoker box. Soak remaining chips in water in medium bowl for 15 to 30 minutes. Drain. Place on top of dry chips. Close smoker box. Place smoker box on 1 side of grill in gas barbecue. Close lid. Heat barbecue to medium for 15 to 20 minutes until chips are smoking. Place chicken on greased grill opposite smoker box. Turn off burner under chicken. Close lid. Cook for about 50 minutes, turning and brushing often with reserved marinade, until no longer pink inside. Makes 36 wing pieces or 24 drumettes.

1 wing: 57 Calories; 3.5 g Total Fat (1.4 g Mono, 0.8 g Poly, 1 g Sat); 16 mg Cholesterol; 2 g Carbohydrate; trace Fibre; 4 g Protein; 79 mg Sodium

WHISPERING WINGS: If you prefer a milder wing, reduce hot pepper sauce to 2 tsp. (10 mL).

Smoked Pepper Steak

A thick, heavily peppered steak with a tender and tasty result.

Mesquite (or hickory) wood chips	1 1/2 cups	375 mL
Water		
Lemon juice	2 tsp.	10 mL
Cooking oil	2 tsp.	10 mL
Worcestershire sauce	1 tsp.	5 mL
Garlic clove, minced (or 1/4 tsp., 1 mL, powder)	1	1
Seasoned salt	1/4 tsp.	1 mL
Top sirloin steak (1 1/2 inches, 3.8 cm, thick), see Note	2 1/4 lbs.	1 k g
Crushed black peppercorns (see Tip, page 66)	2 tbsp.	30 mL

Put 1/2 of dry wood chips into smoker box. Soak remaining chips in water in medium bowl for 15 to 30 minutes. Drain. Place on top of dry chips. Close smoker box. Remove 1 side of grill from gas barbecue. Place smoker box directly on heat source. Replace grill. Close lid. Heat barbecue to medium for 15 to 20 minutes until chips are smoking. Adjust burner under smoker box as necessary to keep it smoking. Adjust opposite burner to maintain medium barbecue temperature.

Combine next 5 ingredients in small bowl. Brush both sides of steak with lemon juice mixture. Firmly press peppercorns into both sides of steak using the heel of your hand or bottom of a glass. Place on greased grill directly over smoker box. Close lid. Cook for 40 minutes, turning once, for medium-rare doneness. For medium or medium-well doneness, increase cooking time by up to 20 minutes. Let stand for 15 minutes before cutting across grain into 1/8 inch (3 mm) slices. Serves 8.

1 serving: 180 Calories; 9.5 g Total Fat (4.3 g Mono, 0.7 g Poly, 3.4 g Sat); 56 mg Cholesterol; 1 g Carbohydrate; trace Fibre; 21 g Protein; 86 mg Sodium

Note: You will need to special order this thickness of steak from your butcher.

Smoky Marinated Salmon

This moist salmon is flavoured with lemon and herbs. Delicious!

Cold water	2 cups	500 mL
Coarse sea salt	2 tbsp.	30 mL
Whole salmon fillet, with skin (about 1 1/2 lbs., 680 g)	1	1
Mesquite (or hickory or maple) wood chips	1 cup	250 mL
Medium lemon	1	1
Lemon pepper	1/4 tsp.	1 mL
Fresh herb sprigs (such as rosemary, thyme, basil, oregano)	4 – 5	4 – 5

Stir water and sea salt in small cup until sea salt is dissolved. Pour into shallow dish large enough to hold salmon fillet. Place fillet, skin-side up, in salt water. Cover. Marinate in refrigerator for at least 4 hours or overnight. Drain. Pat dry with paper towels. Let fillet stand at room temperature, skin-side down, on wire rack for 30 minutes. Pat dry with paper towels. Fillet should be quite dry to the touch before being smoked.

Put dry wood chips into smoker box. Cut several pieces of zest from lemon. Add to smoker box. Cut lemon in half. Squeeze juice from both lemon halves over chips. Close smoker box. Remove 1 side of grill from gas barbecue. Place smoker box directly on heat source. Replace grill. Close lid. Heat barbecue to medium for 15 to 20 minutes until chips are smoking. Adjust burner under smoker box as necessary to keep it smoking. Adjust opposite burner to maintain medium barbecue temperature.

Place fillet, skin-side down, on greased grill directly over smoker box. Sprinkle with lemon pepper. Lay herb sprigs over top. Close lid. Cook for about 15 minutes until fish flakes easily when tested with fork. Cut through flesh and lift salmon from skin to serve. Serves 4.

1 serving: 323 Calories; 19.1 g Total Fat (6.8 g Mono, 6.8 g Poly, 3.9 g Sat); 96 mg Cholesterol; 2 g Carbohydrate; 1 g Fibre; 34 g Protein; 1862 mg Sodium

Maple-Smoked Squash

Very attractive, golden squash filled with a rich, brown bean mixture.

Maple wood chips	1 1/2 cups	375 mL
Water		
Cooking oil	2 tsp.	10 mL
Medium acorn squash (about 1 1/4 lbs., 560 g, each), cut in half lengthwise and seeded	2	2
Finely chopped onion	1/4 cup	60 mL
Garlic clove, minced (or 1/4 tsp., 1 mL, powder)	1	1
Hard margarine (or butter)	4 tsp.	20 mL
Balsamic vinegar	1 1/2 tbsp.	25 mL
Blackstrap molasses	3 tbsp.	50 mL
Chili sauce	3 tbsp.	50 mL
Can of romano (or mixed) beans, rinsed and drained	19 oz.	540 mL
Chopped pecans (or walnuts), toasted (see Tip, page 146)	2 tbsp.	30 mL

Put 1/2 of dry wood chips into smoker box. Soak remaining chips in water in medium bowl for 15 to 30 minutes. Drain. Place on top of dry chips. Close smoker box. Remove 1 side of grill from gas barbecue. Place smoker box directly on heat source. Replace grill. Close lid. Heat barbecue to medium for 15 to 20 minutes until chips are smoking. Adjust burner under smoker box as necessary to keep it smoking. Adjust opposite burner to maintain medium barbecue temperature.

Brush cooking oil on cut sides of squash. Place, cut side down, on greased grill directly over smoker box. Close lid. Cook for 30 minutes.

Sauté onion and garlic in margarine in large frying pan until onion is soft and starting to brown.

Add vinegar, molasses and chili sauce. Cook until bubbling. Remove from heat.

(continued on next page)

Smoked Dishes

Stir in beans, mashing a few with back of spoon, until thick and combined with sauce. Turn squash, cut side up. Spoon 1/4 of bean mixture into cavity of each squash. Close lid. Cook for about 30 minutes until tender.

Just before serving, sprinkle 1 1/2 tsp. (7 mL) pecans over bean mixture in each squash. Serves 4.

1 serving: 292 Calories; 9.3 g Total Fat (5.5 g Mono, 1.9 g Poly, 1.3 g Sat); 0 mg Cholesterol; 50 g Carbohydrate; 7 g Fibre; 7 g Protein; 382 mg Sodium

Pictured on page 126.

Smoked Sea Scallops

A definite smoky taste in these tender scallops.
The ideal topping for a salad or alone as an appetizer.

Mesquite (or hickory) wood chips	1 cup	250 mL
Water		
Cooking oil	2 tbsp.	30 mL
Lemon juice	2 tbsp.	30 mL
Large sea scallops (about 20)	1 lb.	454 g
Bamboo skewers (8 inch, 20 cm, length), soaked in water for 10 minutes	4	4

Put 1/2 of dry wood chips into smoker box. Soak remaining chips in water in small bowl for 15 to 30 minutes. Drain. Place on top of dry chips. Close smoker box. Remove 1 side of grill from gas barbecue. Place smoker box directly on heat source. Replace grill. Close lid. Heat barbecue to medium for 15 to 20 minutes until chips are smoking. Adjust burner under smoker box as necessary to keep it smoking. Adjust opposite burner to maintain medium-low barbecue temperature.

Mix cooking oil, lemon juice and scallops in small bowl. Marinate at room temperature for 15 minutes.

Thread scallops onto skewers, poking skewers through narrower sides of scallops and leaving broader, flat sides exposed. Arrange on greased grill directly over smoker box. Close lid. Cook for 8 to 10 minutes per side until opaque and nicely grilled. Serves 4.

1 serving: 163 Calories; 7.8 g Total Fat (4.1 g Mono, 2.3 g Poly, 0.6 g Sat); 37 mg Cholesterol; 3 g Carbohydrate; trace Fibre; 19 g Protein; 183 mg Sodium

Smoked Dishes

Warm Potato Salad

This rich potato salad is made in a foil packet on the barbecue.

Medium potatoes, cut into 3/4 inch (2 cm) cubes	4	4
Water		
Bacon slices, cooked crisp and crumbled	4	4
Finely chopped onion	1/3 cup	75 mL
Finely chopped celery	1/4 cup	60 mL
Mayonnaise (not salad dressing)	1/3 cup	75 mL
Sour cream	1/4 cup	60 mL
Apple cider vinegar	3 tbsp.	50 mL
Granulated sugar	1 tbsp.	15 mL
Garlic clove, minced (or 1/4 tsp., 1 mL, powder)	1	1
Dry mustard	1 tsp.	5 mL
Salt	1/2 tsp.	2 mL
Pepper	1/4 tsp.	1 mL

Cook potato in water for about 15 minutes until tender. Drain. Turn into large bowl.

Add bacon, onion and celery. Place mixture in centre of 16 inch (40 cm) length of heavy-duty (or double layer of regular) foil.

Combine remaining 8 ingredients in small bowl. Drizzle over potato mixture. Bring up 2 long sides of foil and seal with double fold. Fold sides in to enclose potato mixture. Preheat gas barbecue to high. Reduce heat to medium-low. Place packet on ungreased grill. Close lid. Cook for about 20 minutes, turning occasionally, until hot. Serves 4.

1 serving: 337 Calories; 21.2 g Total Fat (10.9 g Mono, 5.7 g Poly, 4 g Sat); 23 mg Cholesterol; 32 g Carbohydrate; 3 g Fibre; 6 g Protein; 523 mg Sodium

Pictured on page 53.

Roasted Vegetable Mix

A hearty mixture of roasted root vegetables. Roasting intensifies
the natural flavours of these fresh ingredients.

Medium potatoes, with peel, quartered	5	5
Medium onions, quartered	3	3
Whole baby carrots	36	36
Yellow turnip, peeled and cut into 1 inch (2.5 cm) cubes	2 1/2 cups	625 mL
Hard margarine (or butter)	3 tbsp.	50 mL
Olive (or cooking) oil	1 tbsp.	15 mL
Water	1 tbsp.	15 mL
Garlic cloves, minced (or 1/2 tsp., 2 mL, powder)	2	2
Dried whole oregano	1 tsp.	5 mL
Dried thyme	1 tsp.	5 mL
Dried rosemary, crushed	1 tsp.	5 mL
Seasoned salt	1 tsp.	5 mL
Pepper, heavy sprinkle		

Place first 4 ingredients in large greased roaster or foil pan.

Melt margarine in small saucepan on low. Stir in remaining 8 ingredients. Drizzle over vegetable mixture. Toss until well coated. Cover with lid or foil. Preheat gas barbecue to high. Place roaster on ungreased grill. Reduce burner under roaster to low. Close lid. Cook for about 30 minutes, shaking roaster occasionally, until heated through. Remove lid. Stir. Close lid. Cook for about 30 minutes until vegetables are tender and starting to brown. Serves 6 to 8.

1 serving: 279 Calories; 8.6 g Total Fat (5.5 g Mono, 1 g Poly, 1.6 g Sat); 0 mg Cholesterol; 47 g Carbohydrate; 7 g Fibre; 6 g Protein; 347 mg Sodium

Paré Pointer
Good judgment comes from a bad experience
which comes from bad judgment.

Pineapple And Tomato Skewers

These bright, colourful skewers taste as good as they look!
Their fresh, summery flavours and attractive appearance will be a hit!

MARINADE

Cooking oil	3 tbsp.	50 mL
White wine vinegar	3 tbsp.	50 mL
Brown sugar, packed	2 tbsp.	30 mL
Chili sauce	2 tbsp.	30 mL
Garlic salt	1 tsp.	5 mL
Dried whole oregano	1 tsp.	5 mL
Ground allspice	1/4 tsp.	1 mL
Fresh pineapple, peeled and cut into 3/4 inch (2 cm) cubes	1	1
Cherry tomatoes (about 3 cups, 750 mL)	24	24
Medium zucchini, with peel, cut into 1/2 inch (12 mm) thick slices	2	2
Bamboo skewers (10 inch, 25 cm, length), soaked in water for 10 minutes	8	8

Marinade: Combine first 7 ingredients in large bowl or resealable freezer bag.

Add pineapple, tomatoes and zucchini. Stir to coat. Cover or seal. Marinate in refrigerator for 1 to 2 hours.

Thread pineapple, tomatoes and zucchini alternately onto skewers. Preheat electric grill for 5 minutes or gas barbecue to medium. Cook on greased grill for about 15 minutes, turning and brushing with marinade occasionally, until vegetables are tender-crisp and pineapple is browned. Makes 8 skewers.

1 skewer: 111 Calories; 5.7 g Total Fat (3.1 g Mono, 1.7 g Poly, 0.4 g Sat); 0 mg Cholesterol; 16 g Carbohydrate; 2 g Fibre; 1 g Protein; 214 mg Sodium

Pictured on front cover.

Veggie Bread Kabobs

*Crisp, colourful vegetables and crispy cubes of
bread combine to make these wonderful kabobs.*

Medium zucchini, with peel, cut into 1/2 inch (12 mm) thick slices	2	2
Fresh medium mushrooms, halved	16	16
Medium red peppers, cut into 1 inch (2.5 cm) pieces	2	2
Sourdough bread loaf, cut into 1 inch (2.5 cm) cubes	1	1
Bamboo skewers (10 inch, 25 cm, length), soaked in water for 10 minutes	10	10
SAUCE		
Olive (or cooking) oil	1/3 cup	75 mL
Balsamic vinegar	3 tbsp.	50 mL
Sun-dried tomatoes, drained	2 tbsp.	30 mL
Coarsely chopped fresh parsley (or 1 1/2 tsp., 7 mL, flakes)	2 tbsp.	30 mL
Liquid honey	1 tbsp.	15 mL
Garlic clove (or 1/4 tsp., 1 mL, powder)	1	1
Salt	1/4 tsp.	1 mL

Thread zucchini, with cut side facing up, mushrooms, red pepper and bread alternately onto skewers. Place in shallow dish.

Sauce: Put remaining 7 ingredients into blender. Process until smooth. Makes about 3/4 cup (175 mL) sauce. Brush over skewers. Cover. Let stand for 30 minutes. Preheat electric grill for 5 minutes or gas barbecue to medium. Cook skewers on greased grill for about 15 minutes, turning occasionally, until bread is crisp and vegetables are tender. Makes 10 kabobs.

1 kabob: 222 Calories; 9.2 g Total Fat (6.2 g Mono, 1.1 g Poly, 1.4 g Sat); 0 mg Cholesterol; 31 g Carbohydrate; 3 g Fibre; 5 g Protein; 354 mg Sodium

Pictured on page 72.

Side Dishes

Barbecued Asparagus

These tender-crisp asparagus spears are very appetizing.

Vanilla (or plain) yogurt (not non-fat)	1/4 cup	60 mL
White vinegar	1/2 tsp.	2 mL
Lemon pepper	2 tsp.	10 mL
Cooking oil	1/2 tsp.	2 mL
Fresh asparagus, trimmed of tough ends (choose medium thickness, same-sized stalks)	1 lb.	454 g

Stir yogurt, vinegar, lemon pepper and cooking oil in small cup.

Preheat electric grill for 5 minutes or gas barbecue to medium. Arrange asparagus side by side, crosswise to grilling rack, on greased grill. Brush with sauce. Cook for 2 minutes. Coat with more sauce, brushing in 1 direction, pushing asparagus slightly so they roll about 1/4 turn. Cook for 1 to 2 minutes. Repeat brushing and rolling asparagus 2 more times until glazed and tender-crisp. Serves 6.

1 serving: 27 Calories; 0.7 g Total Fat (0.3 g Mono, 0.2 g Poly, 0.2 g Sat); 1 mg Cholesterol; 4 g Carbohydrate; 1 g Fibre; 2 g Protein; 9 mg Sodium

Pictured on page 71.

1. Sweet Pineapple Burgers, page 102
2. Super-Seasoned Spuds, page 106

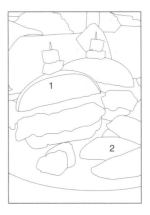

Cinnamon Butter Yams

Soft, glazed yam slices baked in butter and
a nice mixture of warm, comforting spices.

Yam, cut into 1 inch (2.5 cm) thick slices	1 1/4 lbs.	560 g
Boiling water		
Butter (or hard margarine), softened	3 tbsp.	50 mL
Brown sugar, packed	1 tbsp.	15 mL
Ground cinnamon	1/4 tsp.	1 mL
Ground nutmeg	1/4 tsp.	1 mL
Salt	1/4 tsp.	1 mL
Pepper	1/4 tsp.	1 mL

Cook yam in boiling water for 8 to 10 minutes until starting to soften. Drain well. Arrange in 8 inch (20 cm) greased foil pie plate.

Combine remaining 6 ingredients in small bowl. Dollop butter mixture over yam. Cover with foil. Preheat gas barbecue to medium-low. Place pie plate on ungreased grill. Close lid. Cook yam for 10 minutes. Remove foil. Turn yam. Close lid. Cook for 10 to 15 minutes until yam is lightly browned and glazed. Serves 4.

1 serving: 179 Calories; 3.2 g Total Fat (0.9 g Mono, 0.2 g Poly, 1.9 g Sat); 8 mg Cholesterol; 36 g Carbohydrate; 5 g Fibre; 2 g Protein; 190 mg Sodium

Pictured on page 143.

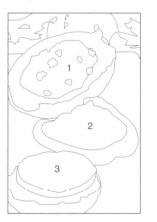

1. Maple-Smoked Squash, page 118
2. Stuffed Peppers, page 132
3. Stuffed Portobello Entree, page 99

Props Courtesy Of: Cherison Enterprises Inc.

Corn And Dill Squash

Tender squash mixed with sweet corn and fresh dill.
A wonderful addition to any barbecued meal.

Butternut squash, cut into 3/4 inch (2 cm) cubes	1 1/2 lbs.	680 g
Hard margarine (or butter)	3 tbsp.	50 mL
Can of kernel corn, drained	12 oz.	341 mL
Chopped fresh chives (or 1 1/2 tsp., 7 mL, dried)	2 tbsp.	30 mL
Honey mustard	1 tbsp.	15 mL
Chopped fresh dill (or 3/4 tsp., 4 mL, dill weed)	1 tbsp.	15 mL
Salt	1/2 tsp.	2 mL
Pepper	1/4 tsp.	1 mL

Divide squash among four 12 inch (30 cm) sheets of greased heavy-duty (or double layer of regular) foil.

Melt margarine in medium saucepan. Remove from heat. Add remaining 6 ingredients. Mix well. Divide corn mixture among squash. Bring up 2 long sides of foil and seal with double fold. Fold sides in to enclose. Preheat gas barbecue to medium-low. Place packets on ungreased grill. Close lid. Cook for about 30 minutes, turning occasionally, until squash is tender. Serves 4.

1 serving: 210 Calories; 9.4 g Total Fat (5.8 g Mono, 1.2 g Poly, 1.9 g Sat); 0 mg Cholesterol; 33 g Carbohydrate; 4 g Fibre; 4 g Protein; 636 mg Sodium

Pesto Zucchini

A quick and easy recipe that goes well with barbecued steak or poultry and potato salad. You can also chop the cooked zucchini and add it to a garden salad for a special treat.

SAUCE
Basil pesto	1/4 cup	60 mL
Balsamic vinegar	2 tbsp.	30 mL
Olive (or cooking) oil	2 tbsp.	30 mL
Liquid honey	2 tbsp.	30 mL
Salt	1/4 tsp.	1 mL
Pepper	1/8 tsp.	0.5 mL

(continued on next page)

Side Dishes

Small green zucchini, with peel, cut lengthwise into 1/4 inch (6 mm) thick slices	2	2
Small yellow zucchini, with peel, cut lengthwise into 1/4 inch (6 mm) thick slices	2	2

Sauce: Combine first 6 ingredients in small bowl. Makes 2/3 cup (150 mL) sauce.

Brush sauce onto both sides of zucchini slices. Preheat electric grill for 5 minutes or gas barbecue to medium. Cook on greased grill for 3 to 4 minutes per side until browned and tender-crisp. Serves 4.

1 serving: 155 Calories; 11.6 g Total Fat (8.4 g Mono, 1.1 g Poly, 1.6 g Sat); 0 mg Cholesterol; 14 g Carbohydrate; 2 g Fibre; 2 g Protein; 153 mg Sodium

Blue Cheese Portobello

Earthy-looking stuffed mushrooms flavoured with blue cheese and an assortment of nuts. Add more barbecue sauce if desired.

Portobello mushrooms (4 inch, 10 cm, diameter)	4	4
Barbecue sauce (your choice)	2 tbsp.	30 mL
Blue cheese, crumbled	3 oz.	85 g
Pine nuts, toasted (see Tip, page 146) and chopped	3 tbsp.	50 mL
Pecans, toasted (see Tip, page 146) and chopped	1/4 cup	60 mL
Chopped fresh parsley (or 3/4 tsp., 4 mL, flakes)	1 tbsp.	15 mL

Scrape away and discard black gills from inside mushrooms. Brush inside with barbecue sauce.

Combine remaining 4 ingredients in small bowl. Divide and spoon into each mushroom. Preheat gas barbecue to medium-high. Place mushrooms on greased grill. Close lid. Cook for 5 to 7 minutes until tender. Serves 4.

1 serving: 194 Calories; 15.8 g Total Fat (6.5 g Mono, 3.3 g Poly, 5.1 g Sat); 16 mg Cholesterol; 8 g Carbohydrate; 3 g Fibre; 9 g Protein; 365 mg Sodium

Grilled Polenta And Salad

Two side dishes—a salad and a bread—to complement any meal.

TOMATO POLENTA

Prepared vegetable broth (or water)	4 cups	1 L
Yellow cornmeal	1 1/2 cups	375 mL
Feta cheese, crumbled	3 oz.	85 g
Finely grated fresh Parmesan cheese	1/4 cup	60 mL
Sun-dried tomato pesto	2 tbsp.	30 mL
Olive (or cooking) oil	1 tbsp.	15 mL

SPINACH AND MUSHROOM SALAD

Olive (or cooking) oil	1 tbsp.	15 mL
Fresh brown (or white) mushrooms, sliced	7 oz.	200 g
Bag of baby spinach leaves	6 oz.	170 g
Pecans, toasted (see Tip, page 146) and coarsely chopped	1/3 cup	75 mL

DRESSING

Olive (or cooking) oil	3 tbsp.	50 mL
Red wine vinegar	1 1/2 tbsp.	25 mL
Chopped fresh parsley (or 3/4 tsp., 4 mL, flakes)	1 tbsp.	15 mL
Granulated sugar	2 tsp.	10 mL
Chili powder	1/4 tsp.	1 mL
Garlic clove, minced (or 1/4 tsp., 1 mL, powder)	1	1

Tomato Polenta: Put broth into large saucepan. Bring to a boil. Reduce heat to medium. Add cornmeal in steady stream, stirring constantly. Cook for about 20 minutes, stirring constantly, until mixture is thick and leaves side of saucepan.

Add next 3 ingredients. Stir. Spread in greased 9 x 9 inch (22 x 22 cm) pan. Chill for about 2 hours until set.

Remove from pan. Cut into 4 squares. Cut each square in half diagonally. Brush each piece with olive oil. Preheat electric grill for 5 minutes or gas barbecue to medium. Cook polenta on well-greased grill for about 5 minutes per side until grill marks appear and polenta is hot. Serves 4.

(continued on next page)

Side Dishes

Spinach And Mushroom Salad: Toss olive oil and mushrooms in medium bowl. Cook mushrooms directly on greased electric grill or in foil pan on barbecue for about 5 minutes until just cooked.

Put mushrooms, spinach and pecans into large bowl. Toss.

Dressing: Combine remaining 6 ingredients in jar with tight-fitting lid. Shake well. Makes 1/3 cup (75 mL) dressing. Drizzle over spinach mixture. Toss. Divide and arrange polenta and salad on 4 salad plates. Serves 4.

1 serving: 566 Calories; 33.1 g Total Fat (19.3 g Mono, 4 g Poly, 7.9 g Sat); 25 mg Cholesterol; 53 g Carbohydrate; 5 g Fibre; 17 g Protein; 1245 mg Sodium

Pictured on page 36.

Corn Grill

These mildly flavoured corncobs are cooked in the husks so they stay tender and moist. Buy the youngest corn available.

Young corncobs in husk	6	6
Hard margarine (or butter), softened	3 tbsp.	50 mL
Paprika	1 1/2 tsp.	7 mL
Onion salt	3/4 tsp.	4 mL
Pepper, heavy sprinkle		
Cold water, to cover		

Pull back husks from corncobs, but don't remove. Pull off silk and discard.

Mix margarine, paprika, onion salt and pepper in small dish. Spread about 1 1/2 tsp. (7 mL) over each cob. Pull husks back up. Secure husks with 2 pieces butcher's string.

Soak in cold water, weighted with plate to submerge, in large container for at least 15 minutes or up to several hours. Drain well. Preheat gas barbecue to medium. Place cobs on greased grill. Close lid. Cook for about 30 minutes, turning 3 or 4 times, until husks are browned and corn is tender. Makes 6 corncobs.

1 corncob: 184 Calories; 7.4 g Total Fat (4.2 g Mono, 1.4 g Poly, 1.4 g Sat); 0 mg Cholesterol; 31 g Carbohydrate; 5 g Fibre; 4 g Protein; 237 mg Sodium

Stuffed Peppers

Beautifully cooked peppers with a rich, creamy ham filling.
The cheesy aftertaste is delicious.

ZUCCHINI HAM STUFFING

Olive (or cooking) oil	1 tbsp.	15 mL
Finely chopped red onion	1/2 cup	125 mL
Garlic cloves, minced (or 1/2 tsp., 2 mL, powder)	2	2
Chili powder	1/2 tsp.	2 mL
Finely chopped zucchini, with peel	1 cup	250 mL
Finely chopped ham	1/3 cup	75 mL
Block of cream cheese, finely chopped	4 oz.	125 g
Finely grated fresh Parmesan cheese	1/4 cup	60 mL
Chopped fresh sweet basil (or 3/4 tsp., 4 mL, dried)	1 tbsp.	15 mL
Medium red pepper, cut in half lengthwise	1	1
Medium yellow pepper, cut in half lengthwise	1	1

Zucchini Ham Stuffing: Heat olive oil in medium frying pan on medium-low. Cook red onion, garlic and chili powder for about 10 minutes, stirring occasionally, until onion is soft.

Add zucchini. Increase heat to medium. Cook for about 5 minutes until zucchini is tender. Remove from heat. Cool for 10 minutes.

Add next 4 ingredients. Stir. Makes 1 1/3 cups (325 mL) stuffing.

Divide and spoon stuffing into each pepper half. Preheat gas barbecue to medium. Place stuffed peppers on ungreased baking sheet or in foil pan. Set on ungreased grill. Close lid. Cook for about 15 minutes until peppers are soft and slightly blackened. Serves 4.

1 serving: 229 Calories; 17.7 g Total Fat (6.7 g Mono, 1 g Poly, 9 g Sat); 47 mg Cholesterol; 10 g Carbohydrate; 2 g Fibre; 9 g Protein; 407 mg Sodium

Pictured on page 126.

Grilled Cake And Strawberries

Soft, grilled cake slices topped with strawberries and cream.
This lemon-flavoured cake not only looks good, it tastes heavenly!

Maple (or maple-flavoured) syrup	1/2 cup	125 mL
Prepared orange juice	1/3 cup	75 mL
Hard margarine (or butter), melted	2 tbsp.	30 mL
Finely grated lemon zest	1 tsp.	5 mL
Frozen pound cake, thawed	10 1/2 oz.	298 g
STRAWBERRY TOPPING		
Lemon curd	1/2 cup	125 mL
Whipping (or half-and-half) cream	2 tbsp.	30 mL
Fresh strawberries, cut in half (or quartered if large)	3 cups	750 mL

Combine first 4 ingredients in shallow dish.

Cut crust off cake. Cut into 6 slices crosswise. Cut each slice in half diagonally. Dip all sides of each piece into maple syrup mixture. Preheat electric grill for 5 minutes or gas barbecue to medium. Cook cake on well-greased grill for about 3 minutes per side until grill marks appear.

Strawberry Topping: Combine lemon curd and whipping cream in small saucepan. Heat and stir on medium for about 3 minutes until lemon curd is melted. Cool slightly.

Put strawberries into medium bowl. Drizzle with lemon curd mixture. Toss gently to coat. To serve, spoon topping over cake on individual serving plates. Serves 6.

1 serving: 451 Calories; 21.2 g Total Fat (8.5 g Mono, 1.9 g Poly, 9 g Sat); 152 mg Cholesterol; 64 g Carbohydrate; 2 g Fibre; 5 g Protein; 468 mg Sodium

Pictured on page 144.

Pear And Blue Cheese Treat

If you prefer something with a little less sweetness, this is the perfect dessert.

Crumbled blue cheese	1/2 cup	125 mL
Large pita breads (7 inch, 18 cm, diameter)	2	2
Ripe small pears, cut into 8 – 10 slices each	2	2
Chopped dates	1/4 cup	60 mL
Pecans, toasted (see Tip, page 146) and chopped	1/4 cup	60 mL

Sprinkle blue cheese over pitas.

Arrange pear slices in pinwheel pattern over top. Sprinkle with dates and pecans. Preheat gas barbecue to medium. Place pitas on greased grill. Close lid. Cook for 5 to 7 minutes until pitas are crisp and cheese is melted. Makes 2. Serves 4 to 6.

1 serving: 314 Calories; 11.3 g Total Fat (4.8 g Mono, 1.8 g Poly, 3.8 g Sat); 13 mg Cholesterol; 47 g Carbohydrate; 5 g Fibre; 9 g Protein; 477 mg Sodium

Banana Pouches

A warm and inviting treat with sweet bananas and oranges drizzled in a hot rum-flavoured sauce. Serve with ice cream or frozen yogurt.

Firm medium bananas, peeled and cut in half lengthwise	4	4
Can of mandarin orange segments, drained	10 oz.	284 mL
Hard margarine (or butter)	8 tsp.	40 mL
Brown sugar, packed	2 tbsp.	30 mL
Prepared orange juice	1/4 cup	60 mL
Rum flavouring	1/2 tsp.	2 mL

Place 2 banana halves, cut side up, in centre of sheet of heavy-duty (or double layer of regular) foil large enough to enclose bananas. Repeat with remaining bananas.

Divide orange segments over bananas. Dot each with 2 tsp. (10 mL) margarine. Sprinkle each with 1 1/2 tsp. (7 mL) brown sugar.

(continued on next page)

Desserts

Stir orange juice and rum flavouring in small cup. Spoon about 1 tbsp. (15 mL) over each fruit mixture. Fold edges of foil to enclose. Preheat gas barbecue to medium. Place packets on ungreased grill. Close lid. Cook for about 10 minutes until bubbling. Serves 4.

1 serving: 226 Calories; 8.4 g Total Fat (5.1 g Mono, 0.9 g Poly, 1.8 g Sat); 0 mg Cholesterol; 40 g Carbohydrate; 2 g Fibre; 2 g Protein; 95 mg Sodium

BBQ Apples

Just like an oven-baked apple! Filled with pretty red cranberries, brown sugar and a touch of cinnamon. Delicious!

Medium cooking apples (such as McIntosh)	4	4
Hard margarine (or butter), softened	1 tbsp.	15 mL
Brown sugar, packed	1/4 cup	60 mL
Ground cinnamon	1/4 tsp.	1 mL
Chopped fresh (or frozen, thawed) cranberries	3 tbsp.	50 mL

Core apples. Score skin of apples around outside middle with knife. This will prevent the skin from splitting too much. Set each apple on individual sheet of heavy-duty (or double layer of regular) foil large enough to enclose apple.

Cream margarine, brown sugar and cinnamon well. Add cranberries. Mix. Divide and stuff into cavities in apples. Wrap each in foil, sealing well. Preheat gas barbecue to medium. Place packets on ungreased grill. Close lid. Cook for about 30 minutes, turning every 10 minutes, until tender. Serves 4.

1 serving: 165 Calories; 3.4 g Total Fat (1.9 g Mono, 0.4 g Poly, 0.7 g Sat); 0 mg Cholesterol; 36 g Carbohydrate; 3 g Fibre; trace Protein; 40 mg Sodium

Paré Pointer

She has never seen a catfish. Actually, she knows that cats don't fish.

Balsamic Peaches

Fresh, glazed peaches with visible grill marks. Serve with grilled croissants and this delicious Ginger Ice Cream.

GINGER ICE CREAM

Vanilla ice cream, softened	4 cups	1 L
Finely chopped crystallized ginger	1/2 cup	125 mL
Sliced almonds, toasted (see Tip, page 146)	1/2 cup	125 mL
Ground cinnamon	1/4 tsp.	1 mL
Fresh peaches, with peel, cut in half and pits removed (see Note)	6	6
Balsamic vinegar	1/3 cup	75 mL
Liquid honey, warmed	1/4 cup	60 mL
Croissants, cut in half horizontally	3	3
Hard margarine (or butter), melted	2 tbsp.	30 mL
Fresh raspberries	1/2 cup	125 mL

Ginger Ice Cream: Gently stir first 4 ingredients in large bowl. Do not let ice cream melt. Transfer to plastic container. Freeze for 1 to 2 hours until firm.

Combine peaches and vinegar in large non-metal bowl. Chill for 1 hour, stirring occasionally. Drain peaches.

Preheat electric grill for 5 minutes or gas barbecue to medium. Cook peaches on well-greased grill for about 5 minutes per side, brushing with honey, until browned and grill marks appear.

Brush both sides of croissants with margarine. Cook on greased grill for about 2 minutes per side until crisp and grill marks appear. Divide and arrange croissants, peaches and ice cream on individual serving plates.

Sprinkle with raspberries. Serves 6.

1 serving: 559 Calories; 27.3 g Total Fat (11.3 g Mono, 2.5 g Poly, 11.6 g Sat); 66 mg Cholesterol; 75 g Carbohydrate; 4 g Fibre; 9 g Protein; 377 mg Sodium

Pictured on page 108 and on back cover.

Note: Wash peaches before cutting to remove the majority of the "fuzz." Keeping the skin on helps the peaches stay intact while cooking.

Buttered Pineapple

Juicy, grilled pineapple served with a coconut-flavoured whipped cream.
Leave the skin on the pineapple, as we did, for an interesting effect.

Butter (or hard margarine), melted	3 tbsp.	50 mL
Lemon (or lime) juice	3 tbsp.	50 mL
Liquid honey	2 tbsp.	30 mL
Fresh small pineapple, unpeeled, cut into	1	1
8 slices (about 1/2 inch, 12 mm, thick),		
each slice cut in half		
COCONUT CREAM SAUCE		
Whipping cream	1 cup	250 mL
Icing (confectioner's) sugar	2 tbsp.	30 mL
Coconut-flavoured liqueur (such as Malibu)	2 – 3 tbsp.	30 – 50 mL

Combine first 3 ingredients in small bowl. Brush onto both sides of each pineapple slice. Preheat gas barbecue to medium. Place pineapple on greased grill. Close lid. Cook for 3 to 5 minutes per side, brushing with butter mixture, until browned.

Coconut Cream Sauce: Beat whipping cream and icing sugar in medium bowl until soft peaks form.

Stir in liqueur. Makes about 2 1/3 cups (575 mL) whipped cream. Serve with pineapple. Serves 8.

1 serving: 202 Calories; 15.4 g Total Fat (4.4 g Mono, 0.6 g Poly, 9.4 g Sat); 49 mg Cholesterol; 16 g Carbohydrate; 1 g Fibre; 1 g Protein; 60 mg Sodium

Pictured on page 144.

Fruit Jack

An almost buttery-tasting cake topped with a
generous amount of fruit. A comforting dessert that lends itself
to a dollop of whipped cream or a scoop of ice cream.

All-purpose flour	1 1/4 cups	300 mL
Granulated sugar	1 cup	250 mL
Baking powder	2 tsp.	10 mL
Salt	1/8 tsp.	0.5 mL
Hard margarine (or butter), melted	1/2 cup	125 mL
Milk	3/4 cup	175 mL
Kiwifruit, peeled and sliced	1	1
Sliced fresh strawberries	1 cup	250 mL
Halved seedless grapes	1/2 cup	125 mL

Combine flour, sugar, baking powder and salt in medium bowl. Make a well in centre.

Pour margarine and milk into well. Stir until just moistened. Turn into greased 8 x 8 inch (20 x 20 cm) pan.

Arrange kiwifruit, strawberries and grapes on top. Do not stir. Cover tightly with foil. Preheat gas barbecue to high. Turn off centre or left burner. Place pan on ungreased grill on unlit side. Close lid. Cook for 45 minutes. Remove foil cover. Cook for 30 to 40 minutes until browned and wooden pick inserted in centre comes out clean. Serves 6.

1 serving: 421 Calories; 16.9 g Total Fat (10.6 g Mono, 1.8 g Poly, 3.6 g Sat); 1 mg Cholesterol; 65 g Carbohydrate; 2 g Fibre; 5 g Protein; 382 mg Sodium

 To prevent overcooking, place foods that require a lower heat, such as fruits and vegetables, around the outer edges of a gas barbecue.

Brown Quick Bread

A dark brown, evenly-textured loaf with a slightly sweet molasses taste.
Delicious!

Whole wheat flour	1 1/2 cups	375 mL
All-purpose flour	1 1/2 cups	375 mL
Baking powder	1 tsp.	5 mL
Baking soda	1 tsp.	5 mL
Salt	3/4 tsp.	4 mL
Large egg	1	1
Brown sugar, packed	2 tbsp.	30 mL
Cooking oil	2 tbsp.	30 mL
Milk	1 cup	250 mL
Blackstrap molasses	1/2 cup	125 mL
White vinegar	1 tbsp.	15 mL

Combine first 5 ingredients in large bowl. Make a well in centre.

Beat egg, brown sugar and cooking oil in medium bowl. Add milk, molasses and vinegar. Beat slowly until blended. Pour into well. Stir until just moistened. Turn into greased 9 x 5 x 3 inch (22 x 12.5 x 7.5 cm) loaf pan. Preheat gas barbecue to medium-high. Turn off centre or left burner. Place pan on unlit side of grill. Close lid. Cook for about 40 minutes until wooden pick inserted in centre comes out clean. Turn out onto wire rack to cool. Cuts into 16 slices.

1 slice: 144 Calories; 2.6 g Total Fat (1.2 g Mono, 0.7 g Poly, 0.4 g Sat); 14 mg Cholesterol; 27 g Carbohydrate; 2 g Fibre; 4 g Protein; 234 mg Sodium

Paré Pointer

Whenever you watch a boxing match, there is always one sore loser.

Mexiscones

Spicy, chili-flavoured scones with the sweetness
of cornmeal and a nice, crunchy texture.

All-purpose flour	2 cups	500 mL
Yellow cornmeal	2/3 cup	150 mL
Granulated sugar	2 tbsp.	30 mL
Baking powder	4 tsp.	20 mL
Cream of tartar	1/2 tsp.	2 mL
Chili powder	1/2 tsp.	2 mL
Salt	1/2 tsp.	2 mL
Hard margarine (or butter), cut up	1/2 cup	125 mL
Large egg	1	1
Can of diced green chilies	4 oz.	113 g
Milk	1/3 cup	75 mL
Grated sharp Cheddar cheese	2/3 cup	150 mL

Chili powder, sprinkle

Mix first 7 ingredients in large bowl. Cut in margarine until crumbly.

Beat egg in small bowl with fork. Add green chilies, milk and cheese. Stir. Add to flour mixture. Stir until soft ball forms. Knead 3 times on lightly floured surface. Divide in half. Pat into two 6 inch (15 cm) circles. Place on greased baking sheet that will fit on 1 side of your gas barbecue. Score 8 wedges into each top.

Sprinkle with chili powder. Preheat gas barbecue to high. Turn off centre or left burner. Place baking sheet on unlit side of grill. Close lid. Cook for about 15 minutes until risen and browned. Cuts into 16 wedges.

1 wedge: 172 Calories; 8.3 g Total Fat (4.6 g Mono, 0.8 g Poly, 2.5 g Sat); 19 mg Cholesterol; 20 g Carbohydrate; 1 g Fibre; 4 g Protein; 359 mg Sodium

Pictured on page 54.

Beer Bread

A fabulous, golden loaf with a hint of cinnamon and beer.
Spread with a bit of butter when warm and enjoy!

All-purpose flour	3 cups	750 mL
Granulated sugar	2 tbsp.	30 mL
Baking powder	4 tsp.	20 mL
Salt	1 tsp.	5 mL
Ground cinnamon	1/4 tsp.	1 mL
Can of beer, room temperature	12 1/2 oz.	355 mL
Cooking oil	1 tbsp.	15 mL
Hard margarine (or butter), softened	1 tsp.	5 mL

Measure first 5 ingredients into large bowl. Stir. Make a well in centre.

Pour beer and cooking oil into well. Mix until soft ball forms. Turn into greased 9 x 5 x 3 inch (22 x 12.5 x 7.5 cm) loaf pan. Push to fill corners. Preheat gas barbecue to medium. Turn off centre or left burner. Place pan on unlit side of grill. Close lid. Cook for about 55 minutes until risen and golden.

Brush with margarine. Turn out onto wire rack to cool. Cuts into 16 slices.

*1 slice: 117 Calories; 1.4 g Total Fat (0.7 g Mono, 0.4 g Poly, 0.2 g Sat); 0 mg Cholesterol;
22 g Carbohydrate; 1 g Fibre; 3 g Protein; 245 mg Sodium*

Pictured on page 90.

tip *If you are heating bread, create double protection against direct heat by placing on two baking sheets or a double layer of heavy-duty foil.*

Chocolate Pizza

A decadent dessert with a chocolate cookie crust and a creamy, hot fudge topping. The almond flavouring mellows out the sweetness of the chocolate.

Tube of refrigerated chocolate cookie dough	16 oz.	454 g
Granulated sugar	1 tbsp.	15 mL
Ricotta cheese	2 cups	500 mL
Almond-flavoured liqueur (such as Amaretto)	3 tbsp.	50 mL
Hot fudge ice cream topping	1/4 – 1/3 cup	60 – 75 mL
Sour cream	1/4 cup	60 mL
Sliced almonds, toasted (see Tip, page 146)	1/3 cup	75 mL
Hot fudge ice cream topping	2 – 3 tbsp.	30 – 50 mL

Press cookie dough in 12 inch (30 cm) ungreased pizza pan. Sprinkle with sugar. Preheat gas barbecue to high. Turn off centre or left burner. Place pan on unlit side of grill. Close lid. Cook for about 10 minutes until crisp. Cool.

Put next 4 ingredients into food processor. Process until smooth. Spread over crust.

Sprinkle with almonds. Drizzle with second amount of ice cream topping. Cuts into 12 wedges.

1 wedge: 356 Calories; 18.7 g Total Fat (7.9 g Mono, 1.9 g Poly, 7.9 g Sat); 36 mg Cholesterol; 38 g Carbohydrate; trace Fibre; 8 g Protein; 145 mg Sodium

Pictured on page 144.

1. Peach Melba Cobbler, page 149
2. Cinnamon Butter Yams, page 127
3. Shrimp On Sole, page 86

Props Courtesy Of: Barbecue Country
The Bay

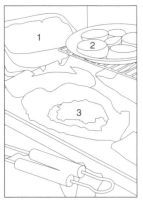

Cookie Pizza

The kids will love the taste of this sweet, soft, giant cookie.
A great treat that will satisfy a large crowd.

Hard margarine (or butter), softened	1 cup	250 mL
Brown sugar, packed	1 cup	250 mL
Large egg	1	1
Vanilla	1/2 tsp.	2 mL
Salt	1/2 tsp.	2 mL
All-purpose flour	2 1/2 cups	625 mL
Baking soda	1 tsp.	5 mL
Currants (or chopped raisins)	1 cup	250 mL
Chopped glazed cherries	1 cup	250 mL
Chopped walnuts (or pecans)	1/2 cup	125 mL
Medium coconut	1/2 cup	125 mL

Cream margarine and brown sugar in large bowl. Add egg, vanilla and salt. Beat until blended.

Sprinkle with flour and baking soda. Stir until just moistened.

Stir in currants, cherries, walnuts and coconut. Press evenly in greased 12 inch (30 cm) pizza pan. Preheat gas barbecue to high. Turn off centre or left burner. Place pan on unlit side of grill. Close lid. Cook for 25 to 30 minutes until edges are golden. Cuts into 20 wedges.

1 wedge: 283 Calories; 13.5 g Total Fat (6.9 g Mono, 2.3 g Poly, 3.6 g Sat); 11 mg Cholesterol; 39 g Carbohydrate; 1 g Fibre; 3 g Protein; 246 mg Sodium

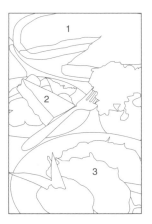

1. Chocolate Pizza, page 142
2. Grilled Cake And Strawberries, page 133
3. Buttered Pineapple, page 137

Props Courtesy Of: Mikasa Home Store
Sears Canada

Rhubarb Custard Pie

*Have you ever thought of baking an old-fashioned pie on the barbecue?
Once you taste this creamy, tart filling and golden, flaky crust,
you'll wonder why you didn't try it sooner!*

**Pastry for 2 crust 9 inch (22 cm) pie,
your own or a mix**

Granulated sugar	1 cup	250 mL
All-purpose flour	3 tbsp.	50 mL
Large eggs	2	2
Milk	1/4 cup	60 mL
Fresh rhubarb, cut into 1/2 inch (12 mm) pieces	3 cups	750 mL
Granulated sugar	1/4 – 1/2 tsp.	1 – 2 mL

Roll out large 1/2 of pastry on lightly floured surface. Fit into 9 inch
(22 cm) pie plate.

Stir first amount of sugar and flour in large bowl. Beat in eggs and milk
until smooth.

Add rhubarb. Stir well. Turn into prepared pie shell. Spread evenly.
Dampen edge with water. Roll out remaining 1/2 of pastry. Lay over top of
pie. Trim and crimp edge to seal. Cut vents in top. Place on ungreased
baking sheet.

Sprinkle with second amount of sugar. Preheat gas barbecue to high. Place
pie on ungreased grill. Close lid. Turn burner under pie to low and leave
opposite burner on high. Cook for about 70 minutes, rotating pie at
halftime, until rhubarb is tender and crust is golden. Cuts into 8 wedges.

*1 wedge: 308 Calories; 11.8 g Total Fat (5.5 g Mono, 1.5 g Poly, 3.8 g Sat); 54 mg Cholesterol;
47 g Carbohydrate; trace Fibre; 4 g Protein; 227 mg Sodium*

 *To toast nuts and seeds, place in ungreased shallow pan. Bake in
350°F (175°C) oven for 5 to 10 minutes, stirring or shaking often,
until desired doneness.*

Apple Raspberry Pie

You can still bake pies on a hot day—use the barbecue and you won't heat up the house. This sweet pie has a rich, burgundy filling that holds its shape well and cuts easily.

Pastry for 2 crust 9 inch (22 cm) pie,
  your own or a mix

Granulated sugar	3/4 cup	175 mL
Minute tapioca	3 tbsp.	50 mL
Ground cinnamon	1/4 tsp.	1 mL
Peeled and sliced cooking apples (such as McIntosh)	2 2/3 cups	650 mL
Raspberries (fresh or frozen)	1 1/2 cups	375 mL
Granulated sugar	1/4 tsp.	1 mL

Roll out large 1/2 of pastry on lightly floured surface. Fit into 9 inch (22 cm) pie plate.

Mix next 3 ingredients in large bowl.

Add apples and raspberries. Stir well. Turn into prepared pie shell. Spread evenly. Dampen edge with water. Roll out remaining 1/2 of pastry. Lay over top of pie. Trim and crimp edge to seal. Cut vents in top. Place on ungreased baking sheet.

Sprinkle with second amount of sugar. Preheat gas barbecue to high. Place pie on ungreased grill. Close lid. Turn burner under pie to low and leave opposite burner on high. Cook for about 70 minutes, rotating pie at halftime, until apple is tender and crust is golden. Cuts into 8 wedges.

1 wedge: 286 Calories; 10.6 g Total Fat (5 g Mono, 1.4 g Poly, 3.4 g Sat); 0 mg Cholesterol; 47 g Carbohydrate; 2 g Fibre; 2 g Protein; 205 mg Sodium

Paré Pointer

He really wanted the job of a chimney sweep.
The boss said, "soot yourself."

Fruit Crisp

Colourful pieces of fruit combined with a sweet crumble mixture.
Scoop out and serve with ice cream when warm,
or allow mixture to cool and cut into pieces.

Hard margarine (or butter)	1/3 cup	75 mL
All-purpose flour	3/4 cup	175 mL
Rolled oats (not instant)	1/2 cup	125 mL
Brown sugar, packed	1/2 cup	125 mL
Ground cinnamon	1/2 tsp.	2 mL
Fresh blueberries	1 cup	250 mL
Fresh raspberries	1 cup	250 mL
Fresh blackberries	1 cup	250 mL
Pecans, toasted (see Tip, page 146) and coarsely chopped	1/2 cup	125 mL
Granulated sugar	1/3 cup	75 mL
Water	1/4 cup	60 mL
Cornstarch	1 tbsp.	15 mL

Melt margarine in medium saucepan on medium. Add next 4 ingredients. Stir. Sprinkle 1/2 of mixture over bottom of greased 8 × 8 inch (20 × 20 cm) pan.

Sprinkle next 4 ingredients over flour mixture.

Combine remaining 3 ingredients in small bowl. Pour over fruit mixture. Sprinkle with remaining 1/2 of flour mixture. Preheat gas barbecue to medium-low. Place pan on ungreased grill. Close lid. Cook for about 30 minutes until fruit mixture bubbles and topping is lightly browned. Serves 6 to 8.

1 serving: 420 Calories; 18.7 g Total Fat (11.5 g Mono, 3.1 g Poly, 2.9 g Sat); 0 mg Cholesterol; 62 g Carbohydrate; 5 g Fibre; 4 g Protein; 135 mg Sodium

 To ensure that food will not be burned, and for safety reasons, keep oven mitts or pot holders in clear sight near the outdoor barbecue for those last-minute melts and unpredictable flare-ups.

Peach Melba Cobbler

A tangy blend of fruit topped with golden, pillowy biscuits.
This soft, juicy dessert will warm you from the inside out.

Frozen sliced peaches	3 1/2 cups	875 mL
Frozen whole raspberries	2 cups	500 mL
Granulated sugar	1 cup	250 mL
All-purpose flour	1 1/2 cups	375 mL
Granulated sugar	2 tbsp.	30 mL
Baking powder	1 tbsp.	15 mL
Salt	1/2 tsp.	2 mL
Hard margarine (or butter)	1/4 cup	60 mL
Milk	3/4 cup	175 mL

Put peaches and raspberries into ungreased 8 × 8 inch (20 × 20 cm) pan. Sprinkle with first amount of sugar. Cover tightly with foil. Preheat gas barbecue to high. Place pan on ungreased grill. Turn burner under pan to low and leave opposite burner on high. Close lid. Cook for 35 to 40 minutes until hot.

Stir next 4 ingredients in medium bowl. Cut in margarine until crumbly.

Add milk. Stir until just moistened. Remove fruit mixture from barbecue, closing lid to preserve temperature inside. Remove foil cover. Drop batter by tablespoonfuls over hot fruit. Return to barbecue. Cook, uncovered, for about 30 minutes until browned and wooden pick inserted in centre of topping comes out clean. Serves 6.

1 serving: 596 Calories; 9.1 g Total Fat (5.5 g Mono, 1.1 g Poly, 2 g Sat); 1 mg Cholesterol; 127 g Carbohydrate; 7 g Fibre; 6 g Protein; 505 mg Sodium

Pictured on page 143.

Measurement Tables

Throughout this book measurements are given in Conventional and Metric measure. To compensate for differences between the two measurements due to rounding, a full metric measure is not always used. The cup used is the standard 8 fluid ounce. Temperature is given in degrees Fahrenheit and Celsius. Baking pan measurements are in inches and centimetres as well as quarts and litres. An exact metric conversion is given below as well as the working equivalent (Metric Standard Measure).

Oven Temperatures

Fahrenheit (°F)	Celsius (°C)
175°	80°
200°	95°
225°	110°
250°	120°
275°	140°
300°	150°
325°	160°
350°	175°
375°	190°
400°	205°
425°	220°
450°	230°
475°	240°
500°	260°

Pans

Conventional Inches	Metric Centimetres
8x8 inch	20x20 cm
9x9 inch	22x22 cm
9x13 inch	22x33 cm
10x15 inch	25x38 cm
11x17 inch	28x43 cm
8x2 inch round	20x5 cm
9x2 inch round	22x5 cm
10x4 1/2 inch tube	25x11 cm
8x4x3 inch loaf	20x10x7.5 cm
9x5x3 inch loaf	22x12.5x7.5 cm

Spoons

Conventional Measure	Metric Exact Conversion Millilitre (mL)	Metric Standard Measure Millilitre (mL)
1/8 teaspoon (tsp.)	0.6 mL	0.5 mL
1/4 teaspoon (tsp.)	1.2 mL	1 mL
1/2 teaspoon (tsp.)	2.4 mL	2 mL
1 teaspoon (tsp.)	4.7 mL	5 mL
2 teaspoons (tsp.)	9.4 mL	10 mL
1 tablespoon (tbsp.)	14.2 mL	15 mL

Cups

Conventional Measure	Metric Exact Conversion Millilitre (mL)	Metric Standard Measure Millilitre (mL)
1/4 cup (4 tbsp.)	56.8 mL	60 mL
1/3 cup (5 1/3 tbsp.)	75.6 mL	75 mL
1/2 cup (8 tbsp.)	113.7 mL	125 mL
2/3 cup (10 2/3 tbsp.)	151.2 mL	150 mL
3/4 cup (12 tbsp.)	170.5 mL	175 mL
1 cup (16 tbsp.)	227.3 mL	250 mL
4 1/2 cups	1022.9 mL	1000 mL (1 L)

Dry Measurements

Conventional Measure Ounces (oz.)	Metric Exact Conversion Grams (g)	Metric Standard Measure Grams (g)
1 oz.	28.3 g	28 g
2 oz.	56.7 g	57 g
3 oz.	85.0 g	85 g
4 oz.	113.4 g	125 g
5 oz.	141.7 g	140 g
6 oz.	170.1 g	170 g
7 oz.	198.4 g	200 g
8 oz.	226.8 g	250 g
16 oz.	453.6 g	500 g
32 oz.	907.2 g	1000 g (1 kg)

Casseroles

CANADA & BRITAIN		UNITED STATES	
Standard Size Casserole	Exact Metric Measure	Standard Size Casserole	Exact Metric Measure
1 qt. (5 cups)	1.13 L	1 qt. (4 cups)	900 mL
1 1/2 qts. (7 1/2 cups)	1.69 L	1 1/2 qts. (6 cups)	1.35 L
2 qts. (10 cups)	2.25 L	2 qts. (8 cups)	1.8 L
2 1/2 qts. (12 1/2 cups)	2.81 L	2 1/2 qts. (10 cups)	2.25 L
3 qts. (15 cups)	3.38 L	3 qts. (12 cups)	2.7 L
4 qts. (20 cups)	4.5 L	4 qts. (16 cups)	3.6 L
5 qts. (25 cups)	5.63 L	5 qts. (20 cups)	4.5 L

Tip Index

Recipe Index

153

154

155

Company's Coming cookbooks are available at retail locations throughout Canada!

EXCLUSIVE mail order offer on next page

Buy any 2 cookbooks—choose a 3rd FREE of equal or lesser value than the lowest price paid.

Original Series — CA$15.99 Canada — US$12.99 USA & International

CODE		CODE		CODE	
SQ	150 Delicious Squares	SF	Stir-Fry	RL	Recipes For Leftovers
CA	Casseroles	MAM	Make-Ahead Meals	EB	The Egg Book
MU	Muffins & More	PB	The Potato Book	SDPP	School Days Party Pack
SA	Salads	CCLFC	Low-Fat Cooking	HS	Herbs & Spices
AP	Appetizers	CFK	Cook For Kids	BEV	The Beverage Book
SS	Soups & Sandwiches	SCH	Stews, Chilies & Chowders	SCD	Slow Cooker Dinners
CO	Cookies	FD	Fondues	WM	30-Minute Weekday Meals
PA	Pasta	RC	The Rookie Cook	SDL	School Days Lunches
BA	Barbecues	RHR	Rush-Hour Recipes	PD	Potluck Dishes
PR	Preserves	SW	Sweet Cravings	GBR	Ground Beef Recipes
CH	Chicken, Etc.	YRG	Year-Round Grilling	FRIR	4-Ingredient Recipes **NEW** May 1/06
KC	Kids Cooking	GG	Garden Greens		
CT	Cooking For Two	CHC	Chinese Cooking		
SC	Slow Cooker Recipes	PK	The Pork Book		

3-in-1 Cookbook Collection

CODE	CA$29.99 Canada US$24.99 USA & International
QEE	Quick & Easy Entertaining

Lifestyle Series

CODE	CA$19.99 Canada US$15.99 USA & International
DC	Diabetic Cooking
DDI	Diabetic Dinners
LCR	Low-Carb Recipes
HR	Easy Healthy Recipes

Most Loved Recipe Collection

CODE	CA$23.99 Canada US$19.99 USA & International
MLA	Most Loved Appetizers
MLMC	Most Loved Main Courses
MLT	Most Loved Treats
MLBQ	Most Loved Barbecuing
MLCO	Most Loved Cookies

CODE	CA$24.99 Canada US$19.99 USA & International
MLSD	Most Loved Salads & Dressings **NEW** March 1/06

Special Occasion Series

CODE	CA$20.99 Canada US$19.99 USA & International
GFK	Gifts from the Kitchen

CODE	CA$24.99 Canada US$19.99 USA & International
BSS	Baking—Simple to Sensational
CGFK	Christmas Gifts from the Kitchen
TR	Timeless Recipes for All Occasions **NEW** April 1/06

Cookbook Author Biography

CODE	CA$15.99 Canada US$12.99 USA & International
JP	Jean Paré: An Appetite for Life **NEW** April 1/06

Company's Coming
COOKBOOKS®

Company's Coming Publishing Limited

2311 – 96 Street
Edmonton, Alberta
Canada T6N 1G3
Tel: 780-450-6223
Fax: 780-450-1857
www.companyscoming.com

Order **ONLINE** for fast delivery!

Log onto **www.companyscoming.com**, browse through our library of cookbooks, gift sets and newest releases and place your order using our fast and secure online order form.

Buy 2, Get 1 FREE!

Buy any 2 cookbooks—choose a **3rd FREE** of equal or lesser value than the lowest price paid.

Title	Code	Quantity	Price	Total
			$	$
DON'T FORGET to indicate your FREE BOOK(S). (see exclusive mail order offer above) please print				

TOTAL BOOKS (including FREE)		TOTAL BOOKS PURCHASED:	$

	International	Canada & USA
Shipping & Handling First Book (per destination)	$ 11.98 (one book)	$ 5.98 (one book)
Additional Books (include FREE books)	$ ($4.99 each)	$ ($1.99 each)
Sub-Total	$	$
Canadian residents add G.S.T.(7%)		$
TOTAL AMOUNT ENCLOSED	$	$

Terms
- All orders must be prepaid. Sorry, no C.O.D.'s
- Prices are listed in Canadian Funds for Canadian orders, or US funds for US & International orders.
- Prices are subject to change without prior notice.
- Canadian residents must pay 7% G.S.T. (no provincial tax required)
- No tax is required for orders outside Canada.
- Satisfaction is guaranteed or return within 30 days for a full refund.
- Make cheque or money order payable to: **Company's Coming Publishing Limited.**
- Orders are shipped surface mail. For courier rates, visit our website: **www.companyscoming.com** or contact us: **Tel: 780-450-6223 Fax: 780-450-1857.**

Gift Giving
- Let us help you with your gift giving!
- We will send cookbooks directly to the recipients of your choice if you give us their names and addresses.
- Please specify the titles you wish to send to each person.
- If you would like to include your personal note or card, we will be pleased to enclose it with your gift order.
- Company's Coming Cookbooks make excellent gifts: birthdays, bridal showers, Mother's Day, Father's Day, graduation or any occasion ...collect them all!

☐ MasterCard   ☐ VISA   Expiry _____ / _____ MO/YR

Credit Card # _____

Name of cardholder _____

Cardholder signature _____

Shipping Address Send the cookbooks listed above to:
☐ **Please check if this is a Gift Order**

Name: _____

Street: _____

City: _____ Prov./State: _____

Postal Code/Zip: _____ Country: _____

Tel: ( ) _____

E-mail address: _____

Your privacy is important to us. We will not share your e-mail address or personal information with any outside party.

☐ **YES! Please add me to your newsletter e-mail list.**

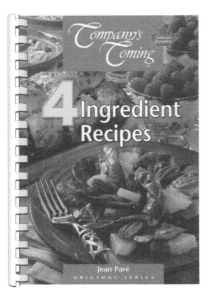

Perfect for your busy family! Make terrific home-cooked meals with just a few convenient products and common ingredients. *4-Ingredient Recipes* offers more than 170 Guaranteed Great ™, all-new recipes for households on the go. Simple to make, delicious to eat!

COOKBOOKS

Quick & Easy Recipes

Everyday Ingredients

Canada's **most popular cookbooks!**